GUIDE TO FAITH

Helmut Harder

Library of Congress Number 79-50682
International Standard Book Number 0-87303-022-2
Printed in the United States of America
Copyright © 1979 by Faith and Life Press
718 Main Street, Newton, Kansas 67114-0347

Design by John Hiebert
Printing by Mennonite Press, Inc.

Second Printing, 1986

Introduction

An orderly outline of the Christian faith has its place in the teaching ministry of the church. There is a time for telling Bible stories; a time for studying church history; a time for discussing relevant issues. But there is also a time for a systematic presentation of what we believe—systematic treatment of the faith that is a summary of the scriptural teachings stated in such a way that it makes sense to the present-day reader.

A comprehensive study of what the church believes becomes especially important at the time when persons are considering believer's baptism and intentional membership in the congregation. The prospect of this momentous step provides an appropriate occasion for reflecting on the major themes and emphases of the Christian faith. The church has the responsibility of outlining in some detail what it is asking its members to say yes to.

Guide to Faith has been prepared for use in church membership classes in the General Conference Mennonite Church. It could serve both as a resource for teachers and as a reader for class members. However, it is hoped as well that the book will be of service beyond the boundaries of the membership class. Since it provides a summary of the Christian faith as interpreted in the Anabaptist-Mennonite stream of the church, it could be helpful to youth and adults of any age and at varying levels of commitment to the Christian faith.

The emphasis in this study is not on providing a final, perfectly refined statement of our faith, but on offering a faithful summary of what the Scriptures teach, while at the same time presenting selected aspects of church history and treating issues raised in the present day.

Even the most refined statement of our beliefs becomes colored by the age in which we live, by a particular language and culture, and by the questions and perceptions of the writer. This explains why catechisms and church membership materials are rewritten from time to time. It is my prayer that *Guide to Faith* may assist the present generation for a time in its quest for faith and fellowship in the church and in its expressions of faithfulness in the wider community.

Helmut Harder

Contents

1/FAITH

*Now faith is the assurance of things hoped for,
the conviction of things not seen. Hebrews 11:1*

Faith is a very important word in Christian life. We cannot get started without it. It takes a decision of faith to begin the Christian pilgrimage. It takes faith to live continuously as a Christian. The future goal of the believer can only be seen through the eyes of faith.

To have faith is to trust. When we trust someone we throw ourselves upon that person's advice. We cannot prove he is right, but we are willing to trust his judgment and to see where it leads us. To have faith is to abandon our life in trust to Jesus Christ.

Every person lives by faith. That is, we all believe in something or in somebody. You cannot live without placing your trust in some object of affection. Among the variety of things we believe in, something usually has priority. Little children usually have complete faith in their parents. Boys and girls will sometimes believe wholeheartedly in a close friend. Youth and adults are often tempted to have complete faith in money or in a job or in a car. In any case, no one can avoid the conscious or unconscious choice of an object of faith.

It is important to think about the faith we live by and to clarify, as much as possible, what the beliefs are that have power over us. What we believe in influences our living from day to day, whether we admit this or not. Not to have clarified, pinpointed, and established our faith only means that we are being guided, unknowingly, by some faith or other. We can, of course, choose not to think about our faith. But this, too, is a step of faith. It means we will trust ourselves to chance or to fate or to our surroundings. Sometimes this is harmless, but at times it is harmful because we are swayed by beliefs which misdirect us. On the other hand, we do have the freedom and the responsibility to make our own decisions about what we will believe in. We can fix our hopes on a goal and thus live by chosen convictions.

For the Christian, the object of trust is God as we know Him through Jesus Christ. To have faith is to rely totally upon Jesus Christ as the One who has shown us the Father. This requires a decision that is both simple and profound. In the succeeding pages of this book we will seek to describe this faith in its simplicity and in its depth.

Where Faith Begins

Usually we think of faith as a human act, as something *we* express toward God. However, faith begins with God, not with us. The Creator took the first step of faith when He created a world and then placed human beings into the world that He had made to care for it. By creating us and entrusting His world to us, God took a step of faith that is beyond our understanding. Our faith is only a response to the faith which God has in us.

The *faith*-fulness of God has continued throughout history and will continue to the end of time. The following biblical passages express this promise: "Know therefore that the Lord your God is God, the *faith*ful God who keeps covenant and steadfast love with those who love him and keep his commandments, to a thousand generations" (Deut. 7:9); "If we confess our sins, he is *faith*ful and just, and will forgive our sins and cleanse us from all unrighteousness" (1 Jn. 1:9). (Italics mine.)

Thus human faith is a joyful response to the faithfulness of God. Because the Father trusts and loves us, we are motivated to have faith in God in return. Our faith in God is a grateful thank-you to His faith in us.

The Bible pictures the life of faith as a contract or covenant made between partners. In the faith-relationship, God is the stronger partner in the sense that He is more patient, more loving, and more faithful than we are. We can rely on Him not to let us down. This does not mean that we will always get what we think we want or need. It does mean that in the end God will do for us what is in keeping with His divine will.

In the meantime it is our responsibility to be faithful as well. Faithfulness to God is outlined in the teachings of the Bible and the Christian church. Faith is expressed by us in two ways. (1) We must humbly respect God as our Creator and Guide rather than worshiping ourselves or some other object in His place. In Romans 11:20 we read: ". . . You stand fast only through faith. So do not become proud, but stand in awe." (2) As we accept love from God, we in turn express love toward our neighbors. ("So faith by itself, if it has no works, is dead"—James 2:17.) It is our duty to be faithful toward one another because God has been faithful toward us.

Fides and Fiducia

Thomas Aquinas, a theologian of the thirteenth century, spoke of two levels of faith. The first is intellectual assent to Christian teachings; the second is trust in the person Jesus Christ. Using Latin terms, he called the first *fides* and the second *fiducia*. The two aspects of faith must not be separated. We base our faith (*fides*) on the teachings of the Christian church. Thus, "faith comes from what is heard" (Rom. 10:17). At the same time, the object of our faith (*fiducia*) is Jesus Christ, for "the righteousness of God has been manifested . . . through faith in Jesus Christ for all who believe" (Rom. 3:21, 22).

Is faith then a matter of a blind yes to a mysterious claim? Is there no evidence for faith? In our modern age there is a tendency among many people to believe only on the basis of evidence: "If you can give me scientific proof for your claims, I will believe you!" We are hesitant to believe something if it does not have the backing of a laboratory experiment. Or, people will insist that in order for them to believe what you say, your statement must "make sense." That is, it must be logical and consistent.

While scientific evidence and sensible thinking play an important role in our search for truth, these are not final authorities for us. A scientific laboratory is not capable of containing the whole of life. Our minds are wonderful instruments, but the universe is much too large to be restricted to our powers of thought. Furthermore, even if we can *understand* large aspects of the created world through laboratory and the mind, we are still unable to *control* the powers that rule the universe within the immeasurable boundaries of space and time.

In the face of the vastness of the universe and the greatness and mystery of God, some theologians have played down any possibility for man to provide evidence for faith. Soren Kierkegaard, theologian and philosopher of the nineteenth century, described life as paradoxical. That is, you could always see a matter from two opposing sides; for every yes there is a no. In the light of this dilemma he took "the leap of faith." He concluded that one must have faith, but from a human point of view such faith will always be claimed in the face of uncertainty and absurdity. Some day, he said, our questions will find answers. In the meantime we can only live in hope.

Kierkegaard was reacting to those so-called orthodox Christians who identified faith with right doctrine, who assumed that your faith was sure and secure if and when you agreed in heart and mind and will with the church's clearly stated teachings of what a person should believe and do. He felt that church people were too easily nodding their sleepy assent to these teachings without making them their own.

Kierkegaard had a point. But so did orthodox Christianity before him. Faith involves the task, on the one hand, of formulating and accepting a creed, a set of beliefs, while, on the other hand, allowing faith in God to pervade one's personal life. This double-sided task is not easy, but it is necessary. For some, the matter of accepting a set of beliefs that is handed down from previous generations becomes a difficult hurdle. Others are ready to say yes to a creed of faith, but do not care to work at its personal appropriation.

Thus there are some "facts" that support our faith—Christian teachings that spell out what we believe. These teachings have been set forth on the basis of the Bible and have guided the life of countless numbers of Christians throughout the centuries. Thus we can trust them as evidence of faith. Can one use them, then, as "proofs"? In one sense, yes; in another sense, no. Our beliefs participate in the truth, but final truth rests in Jesus, "the author and finisher of our faith" (Heb. 12:2, KJV). The final "proof" of Christian faith is Jesus Christ. He cannot be contained in a test tube, yet He can be known through experience. He cannot be proved true or false through logical arguments, yet He makes "good sense." The truth of Christ is known in a personal relationship with Him.

Signs of Faith

According to the Bible, faith has at least some basis in the events of history. Abraham was given a promise (Gen. 12:1-3) and was invited to follow the Lord in faith on the basis of that promise. He believed, in faith, that he would become the father of a great people. While Abraham did not live to see that day, he was given a son as a sign that pointed to the beginning of the greater promise. The birth of Isaac did not mean that Abraham could now exchange his faith for evidence. It did, however, provide a clue that God was living up to His promise. This strengthened Abraham's faith.

The word *sign* occurs about eighty times in the Old Testament and about seventy-three times in the New Testament. In the majority of these occurrences the reference is to signs as acts or events in history whereby God makes himself known to man. The Bible itself is the story of these signs as they become embedded in the tradition of the people of God. We understand God to some extent through signs that have happened during the course of history. It cannot be claimed, of course, that these signs are "bare facts." There is usually a touch of faith and interpretation involved in the biblical description of happenings. Yet personal experiences and larger historical events provide partial evidence for faith. Throughout biblical times and in our personal life there are sufficient signs to give us "the assurance of things hoped for" (Heb. 11:1).

The Community of Faith

While we said above that each person needs to come to grips personally with the question of faith, this should not be overemphasized. In a sense, the church, the Christian community, is the carrier of faith. This is obviously true in the sense that it is the church that formulates and preserves and hands on its teachings to each new generation. Also, it is the church that has given us the Bible.

But there is another sense in which faith is a community affair. The church is sometimes referred to as the community of faith. Its purpose is to give shelter and fellowship to persons who are seeking to strengthen their faith. Its purpose is also to invite persons to faith who do not believe in Jesus Christ. The Mennonite church has been particularly strong in its emphasis upon the communal nature of faith. Christians are not called to a lonely pilgrimage. They are invited to walk hand in hand in a supportive fellowship.

Against this background one can understand the Mennonite emphasis on joining the church. It is rightly argued that becoming a Christian goes hand in hand with seeking Christian fellowship; that baptism and joining the church belong together. We follow the example given in the ministry of the first apostles as recounted in the Book of Acts where the forming of Christian communities was seen as vital to Christian faith.

In Conclusion

Faith is an act which centers on Jesus Christ. God the Father expressed His faith in mankind by sending Jesus to us to tell us He loves us. Jesus taught the content of the faith to His followers in word and deed. We are invited to rely in faith upon the words and work of Jesus: His work of love on the cross, His words of invitation to follow Him, His word of promise that He will be with us in the Spirit and that He will come again in power. His birth, life, death, and resurrection are a sign of the will of God to us. His purpose on earth was to form a faithful community that would carry His ministry to the ends of the earth. All that we have said about faith in this chapter is expressed in Jesus Christ, and is expressible in our response to Him.

TOPICS FOR DISCUSSION
1. The biblical understanding of faith.
2. Biblical illustrations of faith.
3. The relationship between faith and faithfulness.
4. Present-day questions and influences that make faith difficult.
5. Basic principles that guide the Christian in a life of faith.

SELECTED SCRIPTURE PASSAGES
Hebrews 11:1—12:2
Habakkuk 1:1—2:4 (especially 2:4)
Luke 8:22-25, 42b-48
James 2

AIDS TO REFLECTION
"Faith is the state of being ultimately concerned. . . . Faith as ultimate concern is an act of the total personality." Paul Tillich, *The Dynamics of Faith* (New York: Harper & Row, 1958), pp. 1, 4.

"Faith is essentially that which enables us to direct our effort and movement towards a goal not yet attained." Oliver Quick, *Doctrines of the Creed* (London and Glasgow: Collins, 1963), p. 15.

"Faith in God is used by many as a psychological defense mechanism, a lovely make-believe world to which sentimentally they retreat when they do not want to face life's stern realities. Nothing is free from the possibility of burlesque, not even belief in God. But you do not judge music by jazz;

you know there is Mozart. You do not judge architecture by filling stations; you know there is Chartres. No more should you judge religious faith by the weaklings who use it as a cozy retreat." Harry Emerson Fosdick, *Dear Mr. Brown* (New York and Evanston: Harper & Row Publishers, 1961), p. 20.

FOR FURTHER READING

John Powell, *A Reason to Live! A Reason to Die!* Niles, Illinois: Argus Communications, 1972.

Paul Tillich, *Dynamics of Faith.* New York: Harper & Row, 1957.

Paul S. Minear, *Eyes of Faith: A Study in the Biblical Point of View.* Philadelphia: The Westminster Press, 1946.

2/GOD

"*I am who I am.*" *Exodus 3:14*

In the Beginning God

If faith is our starting point for Christian faith and life, then it follows that belief in God is not something we can prove to ourselves or to others in an obvious way. The reality of God must be affirmed through faith. In Jeremiah 29:13, 14, we read, ". . . When you seek me with all your heart, I will be found by you, says the Lord. . . ." There are persons who have experienced a sudden inbreak of the reality of God into their lives even when they seemed not to be seeking for a divine experience. But for most of us, belief in God begins with a "leap of faith" on our part. God dwells in mystery and does not often make a point of communicating in obvious ways through the tangible things of this world.

At the same time, it is not a matter of mustering enough faith so that we can prove the assumption that God exists. The Bible does not consider it essential to prove God's existence. Genesis 1:1 begins with the words "In the beginning God. . . ." God was there before anything else was considered. In Hebrews 11:6 we read, "For whoever would draw near to God must believe that he exists. . . ." Assuming that God is, the Bible deals mainly with the question of faithfulness between man and God. Thus, while faith is an important ingredient in establishing belief in God, revelation is equally important. If God is quite beyond us both in terms of space and of time, then we are the humble receivers of information about Him. This comes to us from beyond our human circle, from the transcendent world of the infinite God.

We must reckon with the fact that many persons in our day deny the existence of God. This is true for the general populace. It is also true for some rather prominent philosophers and scientists of the modern age. Karl Marx, Friedrich Nietzsche, Sigmund Freud, Bertrand Russell, and others questioned the validity of belief in God. Generally speaking, it is not God as such that is called into question by these critics, but rather a certain idea of what they assume God to be like. Marx was disturbed at the way belief in God was being used by the rich to fortify their advantageous position; Nietzsche was critical of the way in which the church used its belief in a judging God to keep the sinner weak; Freud saw religion as providing an escape from the realities of life. The views of God which these thinkers are opposing are warped images of the real God of the Christian faith. An atheist will often set up a certain notion of God and then proceed to make a case against that view. But such a person has missed the point because he or she has failed to understand God in all the richness of the scriptural portrayal.

It is quite common to identify God all too quickly with some human notion we have about Him. While God cannot be readily identified with this or that material object or experience in our lives, He is nonetheless fundamentally related to everything around us and within us. As Paul Tillich has aptly stated, the Christian faith believes that God is "the ground of being." He provides the life-support for everything that lives and moves in the universe. He is the "uncaused cause" of all that exists. Thus we must always seek Him beyond every object in this world and beyond every experience that we have. At the same time, we can claim that the objects in this world and our human experiences participate in the greater reality of God.

The Biblical View of God

The Christian church takes its clues to an understanding of God primarily from its Scriptures, the Bible. The following is a summary of what we find in the Bible concerning our knowledge of God.

1. The Bible claims that there is only one true God. The first commandments read: "I am the Lord your God, who brought you out of the land of Egypt. . . . You shall have no other gods before me" (Ex. 20:2, 3). The temptation of people in biblical times was not to believe in no God at all, but to believe in many gods. This took the form of trusting in the gods of other nations besides the Lord God of Israel. Such misplaced trust had a practical purpose. If you placed your trust in the god of a neighboring nation, then you had the benefit of the powers of that god as well as your own. In case your God appeared to let you down, you could pray to another. The courting of other nations' gods implied that you were not willing to ascribe full wisdom and might to the God of Israel. You were not willing to trust Him with singleness of heart. The Bible speaks against this half-hearted belief and calls, instead, for a firm trust in one God in the face of suffering and physical death as well as in good times.

2. God is the Creator of the universe and all that is in it: "In the beginning God created. . ." (Gen. 1:1). While God stands above the created order, His word is expressed in it: "The heavens are telling

the glory of God, and the firmament proclaims his handiwork" (Ps. 19:1). We cannot find Him in the leaf, the stone, or the cloud, and yet the created world sings His praises. To be sure, not everything in the universe praises God. There are forces within the created order that have served to warp and corrupt the original creation. Nonetheless God sustains His created world in obvious and mysterious ways even today, and promises that He will restore its original purpose in the end: ". . . the earth shall be full of the knowledge of the Lord as the waters cover the sea" (Is. 11:9*b*).

Christians have sometimes expressed the universal greatness of God with the words *omniscient, omnipotent,* and *omnipresent.* His *omniscience* refers to the idea that He knows everything; *omnipotence* means that He is all-powerful; and *omnipresence* means that He can be everywhere at once.

3. God is Lord of the created world. This includes what we call the world of nature as well as the world of man: "The Lord is high above all nations, and his glory above the heavens!" (Ps. 113:4.) As Lord of the created world He expresses His will through it. Referring to the entire created order, the psalmist says:

> Great are the works of the Lord, studied by all who have pleasure in them. Full of honor and majesty is his work, and his righteousness endures for ever. . . . He has shown his people the power of his works, in giving them the heritage of the nations. The works of his hands are faithful and just; all his precepts are trustworthy, they are established for ever and ever. . . (Ps. 111:2, 3, 6-8).

God exercises His lordship over the world through its history. There is a strong emphasis in the Bible on the fact that God has called the universe into being in the past (creation); that He is watching over His created world at present (providence); and that He will establish His glory throughout the universe in a future eternity (consummation). Within this larger scope, particular attention is given to the purpose of God for the history of mankind. Man is placed in the garden for a special purpose (Gen. 1:28); Abraham is appointed to be the father of a people that will in time become a blessing to all mankind (Gen. 12:1-3); Jesus is sent by God to become the Lord of people of all nations (Mt. 28:18, 20): "And Jesus came and said to them, 'All authority in heaven and on earth has been given to me . . . and lo, I am with you always, to the close of the age.' " Thus when we think of God as Ruler of the world, we affirm Him as the Creator in the past, as Sustainer of life in the present, and as the future Consummator of His divine will. God is the Lord of history.

4. God is the ever-present Guide and Comforter of His people. In the Old Testament this characteristic of God is expressed most warmly in the familiar Twenty-third Psalm: "The Lord is my shepherd." A similar text is found in Isaiah 40:11. "He will feed his flock like a shepherd, he will gather the lambs in his arms, he will carry them in his bosom, and gently lead those that are with young." In the New Testament Jesus Christ brings a message of guidance and comfort from His Father to those whom He contacts. When He is about to leave the earth, He promises to send the Holy Spirit as a Counselor who will comfort and guide His children until He comes again (Jn. 14:16, 17, 26).

5. God is the Father of our Lord and Savior, Jesus Christ. Various witnesses testify to this. The New Testament writer John reports that God dwelt among us in flesh in the person of His Son, Jesus Christ (Jn. 1:14). While "no one has ever seen God; the only Son, who is in the bosom of the Father, he has made him known" (1:18). According to Luke, the angel told Mary that the child about to be born of her "will be called holy, the Son of God" (Lk. 1:35). The Roman centurion who saw Jesus die on the cross exclaimed, "Truly this man was the Son of God" (Mk. 15:39). Thus Jesus Christ affords us an insight into the person of God.

6. God relates to us in love, in grace, and in judgment. These three attributes of God are inseparable from each other. They combine to give genuineness to God's relationship to us. Love is the dominant attitude of God. It is evident both in the act of creation and of redemption. The love of God is kept vital both through grace and through judgment. Love cannot be one-sided; it is guided at least to some extent by the response which it receives. If the love of God meets with a negative reaction on the part of the recipient, this cannot be overlooked. Disobedience must either be forgiven or punished. In His attitude of grace, God is ready to forgive a negative response to His love, but repentance on the part of man is a necessary ingredient in the experience of forgiveness for grace to be authentic. If disobedience persists, the only other recourse is

judgment. God does not desire to judge His people, but there is a point at which His love and grace would become meaningless if judgment were not a factor to be reckoned with. Thus God is a God of love, while forgiveness and judgment are elements which lend authenticity to love.

Proving the Existence of God?

Throughout the centuries following biblical times, many attempts have been made to prove the existence of God. We can only offer a brief sketch of these attempts here, together with some evaluation. St. Augustine, a theologian of the fourth century, wisely stated that any rational arguments for God's existence cannot stand on their own. Only after we have affirmed the reality of God with heart and will can we make good use of our reason.

While philosophers and theologians in the Christian tradition have essentially followed St. Augustine's clue, some have expended considerable effort in trying to establish the existence of God on rational grounds. The most impressive attempt was made by Thomas Aquinas in the thirteenth century. His cosmological argument states that the order and design of the natural universe is evidence of the existence of an all-wise Creator. If you would discover an expertly made watch on a desert island, you would conclude that an intelligent person had made it. Similarly, the created universe declares the handiwork of God the Creator.

One of the interesting and wise voices in the discussion of God's existence is the French philosopher Blaise Pascal. He began with the observation that humans have the option of doubting or of believing in God. Faced with this option, is it not better to believe? If one believes and is proven wrong, nothing changes. But if one believes and is proven right, all is gained. Therefore, believe! His position has been called "the great wager."

In our century the late Paul Tillich has suggested that we should not say, "God exists." When we think of something existing, our minds turn to objects in our world. God is not an object among objects. Rather, He is beyond existence; He is the foundation of all existence. While Tillich's discussion becomes somewhat technical, he does make a valid point. It is all too tempting to reduce God to our level when we attempt to establish His existence with our finite minds.

Concluding Thoughts

Are the arguments for God convincing? Do they earn our respect? There are several positive things that can be said. On the one hand, it is impressive that throughout the centuries people have used their minds to think about the existence of God. On the basis of this tradition of thought we can say that thorough rational thinking is not to be excluded from our Christian faith. In fact, it can contribute to the clarification and affirmation of our faith.

On the other hand, we overstep our bounds if we claim that we can prove God's existence on the basis of these arguments. The skeptic says that the thoughts of the mind are an illusion, or that the design of the universe is to be explained by evolution, or that in the end there is no design at all but that the world is to be explained as an accident. The Christian will argue against him, to be sure. But the Christian admits, even at the outset of the argument, that he comes with a viewpoint which assumes the reality of the spiritual world and the necessity of trust in God. Within the context of these assumptions the practice of formulating arguments for God belongs to the practice of spiritual discipline. It is a way of expressing our faith in God through the gift of the mind.

As human beings caught up in the flow of history on the face of our little planet, our focus should be more on understanding the movement of life in which we are involved with God than in attempting to comprehend the nature of God himself. God affects us more in terms of His activity among us than in terms of a static entity somewhere in the beyond. Thus we do well to concentrate on understanding the flow of Spirit life surrounding us rather than on transcending this world in the hope of catching a glimpse of God this side of death and heaven.

TOPICS FOR DISCUSSION

1. Assumptions about God in the Bible.
2. The various names for God in the Bible
3. The Christian belief in God compared to other religions.
4. Why it is important to believe in God both in good times and in bad times.

SELECTED SCRIPTURE PASSAGES
Acts 17:22-31
Psalm 97
Isaiah 40

AIDS TO REFLECTION

"If the extent or intensity of the world's pain and evil were greatly to increase, would this be taken as disproving theism? No; there is no assignable limit to the capacity of religious faith to trust in God despite daunting and apparently contradicting circumstances." John Hick, *Faith and Knowledge* (Glasgow: William Collins Sons & Co., 1974), p. 166f.

"God does not die on the day that we cease to believe in a personal deity, but we die on the day when our lives cease to be illumined by the steady radiance, renewed daily, of a wonder, the source of which is beyond all reason." Dag Hammarskjöld, *Markings* (London: Faber and Faber, 1964), p. 64.

"Do you believe in God the Father, who made the world and upholds and governs it by his fatherly hand? Do you believe that in Jesus God showed his face to men most clearly, and walked among them to draw them tenderly back to himself? Do you believe that God is still alive and active in the world about us, and in our hearts within us? If you believe these things, you believe in the Trinity. Nevin Harner, *I Believe* (Philadelphia: The Christian Education Press, 1950), p. 38.

On a billboard someone had written these words: "God is dead! Signed, Nietzsche." Someone else had the wisdom to add, "Nietzsche is dead! Signed, God."

FOR FURTHER READING
Louis Cassels, *The Reality of God.* Scottdale, Pa.: Herald Press, 1972.
J. B. Phillips, *Your God Is Too Small.* London: Epworth Press, 1952.
John Hick, *The Existence of God.* New York: Macmillan Publishing Co., 1964.

3/REVELATION

"There is a God in heaven who reveals mysteries." Daniel 2:28

It is clear from what has been said in the last chapter that we cannot pull ourselves up to God's level in order to find out what He is like. Rather, our knowledge of God depends upon His initiative. He must disclose himself to us. It is the Christian's claim that God has revealed himself to people on earth in a variety of ways.

At the same time, the Creator has endowed us with the ability to be receptive to His revelation. We have been given sensitive hearts that can receive love and grace from a Higher Being. We have been blessed with minds that can think about God. We have been given the capacity to speak with God, and to speak with one another about God. We have the ability to understand the laws of God and to desire their implementation. Having experienced the love of God, we have been endowed with the capacity to express the love of God to one another. Thus a bridge can be built between God and persons so that there is communication between heaven and earth. While God is the initiator of the dialogue with us, we also play a part in the act of revelation.

Human beings have had a tendency to take their ability to know God too far. When God gave us the ability to think, it was not intended that we should compete with God. Rather, our task is to think His thoughts after Him. When God blessed us with the ability to make wise choices, He did not want us to assume that we could decide right from wrong on our own. Rather, our task is to learn His ways and be directed by His wisdom. We constantly face the task of dedicating our abilities to their source, God, rather than considering ourselves as the source of revelation.

Avenues of Divine Revelation

A study of the various avenues of revelation in the Bible and throughout history suggests the following classifications.

1. The revelation of God is known through His Son, Jesus Christ. In the drama of revelation, Christ occupies center stage. The writer to the Ephesian church states that God the Father

> has made known to us in all wisdom and insight the mystery of his will, according to his purpose which he set forth in Christ as a plan for the fulness of time, to unite all things in him, things in heaven and things on earth (Eph. 1:9, 10).

The deeds and words of Jesus, together with His death and

resurrection, provide an open window through which we can see God's way and will. If we try to ascertain God's will only from what we see in nature or in the opinions of people, we will be confused, since the clues are varied and complex. However, in Christ, as portrayed in the New Testament, we are provided with a framework for God's truth.

2. The revelation of God is known through the life and work of special individuals and groups. The Old Testament tells the amazing story of how the Lord God spoke through the patriarchs (Abram, Isaac, and Jacob), through great leaders (such as Moses and Joshua), through priests and kings and prophets. The same story is told in the New Testament, with the focus on the disciples and the apostles. These individuals helped to form and perpetuate special communities—the people of Israel in the Old Testament and the church of Jesus Christ in the New Testament—which became channels of the revelation of God.

Not everything that was said or done by these individuals and communities was from God. At times these leaders and communities made false claims to revelation. At times they did not listen faithfully to the word of God. In spite of these shortcomings God has chosen to reveal His will through human instruments. He continues to do so today.

Of the various groups that could be mentioned, the church, insofar as it is a faithful group of gathered believers, has been a vital link in discerning the knowledge of God. The church has occupied itself for centuries with the task of rightly interpreting the revelation of God in Christ. At times this has been a simple matter; at other times the task has been more difficult. A right interpretation of the revelation of God through Jesus Christ requires the activity of an ongoing community dedicated to His mission. While it must be maintained that Jesus Christ is Lord of the church, and thus He is the most important avenue of our knowledge of God, the community of believers serves an important function in hearing and discerning the voice of God.

3. The spoken and written word has a prominent place in divine revelation. God spoke to and through the patriarchs; He addressed the community of Israel through Moses; He spoke to the people through their priests; He addressed kings and common folk through the prophets. Finally, God spoke through His Son, the

Word made flesh. In the first chapter of the Gospel of John we read: "In the beginning was the Word, and the Word was with God, and the Word was God. . . . And the Word became flesh and dwelt among us" (Jn. 1:1, 14a). This is an announcement of Jesus Christ as the incarnate (in-fleshed) Word of God.

Revelation as word comes through persons, but it also appears in written form. The function of the written Scriptures is two-sided. First, the Scriptures preserve the historical account of how God has spoken to people in the past. Secondly, the Scriptures cultivate faith in Jesus Christ in every generation. A familiar passage found in Paul's letter to Timothy expresses this two-sided function of the Scriptures:

> But as for you, continue in what you have learned and have firmly believed, knowing from whom you have learned it and how from childhood you have been acquainted with the sacred writings which are able to instruct you for salvation through faith in Christ Jesus. All scripture is inspired by God and profitable for teaching, for reproof, for correction, and for training in righteousness, that the man of God may be complete, equipped for every good work" (2 Tim. 3:14-17).

As Timothy understood these words, the "sacred writings" and "scripture" were the writings of the Old Testament. In his day the New Testament had not yet been formed into a book. The Bible as a whole was completed in the fourth century A.D. From that time onward the Christian church has placed itself under the authority of the Scriptures because the Bible is the trustworthy report of the beginnings and the high points of the revelation of God in history. The present-day Christian church relies heavily upon the Scriptures for a guide to faith and life.

4. God reveals himself in nature. This includes the so-called world of nature as well as human nature. Psalm 19:1 expresses this truth with respect to the world of nature:

> The heavens are telling the glory of God; and the firmament proclaims his handiwork."

In Romans 1:19, 20, the author, referring to what God has revealed from heaven to man, writes:

For what can be known about God is plain to them, because God has shown it to them. Ever since the creation of the world his invisible nature, namely, his eternal power and deity, has been clearly perceived in the things that have been made.

While the reality of God is portrayed only very generally in the created world, and is often squelched by this-worldly anxieties in the human conscience, the attentive listener can hear the word of God addressing us through nature.

5. Finally, the future aspect of revelation must be noted. We do not assume that all we could possibly know and experience of God's truth has become evident to us. The resources for life have been given in the past; but these resources include promises for a yet outstanding future. It is our expectation that God will reveal himself more fully in the future as the promises of the past, especially those given with the resurrection of Christ, press on toward fulfillment in and beyond our present history. The avenues God will use may include all of the above: Jesus Christ, individuals and community, the spoken and written word, as well as nature and history.

Revelation Through Father, Son, and Holy Spirit

Throughout the centuries the Christian church has held to the doctrine of the Trinity, the belief that God reveals himself in a threefold way as Father, Son, and Holy Spirit. The term trinity is not found in the Bible. It is ascribed to Tertullian, an early theologian of the church, who was born about A.D. 160. Since his day the doctrine of the Trinity has proved helpful as a framework within which God can be understood more adequately.

Clues for a threefold awareness of God can be found in the Bible. The Old Testament tends to emphasize the Fatherhood of God; the Gospels (Matthew, Mark, Luke, and John) highlight Jesus Christ as the incarnate Son of God; with Pentecost (Acts 1) the impact of the Holy Spirit upon the church has its beginning. Thus there are three aspects to the religious experience of God in the Bible. But this division should not be carried too far. The three dimensions of the divine are interrelated throughout the Scriptures. There are many references to the "spirit" in the Old Testament, even though its power is not as closely defined as in the latter part of the New Testament. Also the New Testament states that "the word," namely

Jesus Christ, "was in the beginning with God" (Jn. 1:2). Furthermore, the Fatherhood of God continues as a prominent emphasis in
the New Testament as well. Jesus says, "He who has seen me has
seen the Father" (Jn. 14:9).

From earliest times the church has had to deal with the question
of God's threefold nature. The Christian faith is monotheistic; that
is, we affirm only one God. And yet there is the temptation to think
in terms of a tritheism—three gods. How can God be one and three
at the same time? The history of this rather long and complex
discussion can be summed up by saying that through the years
Christian faith has held to its confession of one God who functions
among us in three dimensions. We can even say that God reveals
himself in three "persons" if we remember that behind the English
word *person* there stands the Latin *persona* which means "face" or
"mask." That is, the one God reveals himself to us in three forms.

Is the doctrine of the Trinity important? The answer is yes and no.
On the one hand we must not expect that the Trinity somehow
gives us inner knowledge into the mathematical composition of
God. God is a living, active Person who cannot be contained in a
discussion of whether He is "three-in-one" or "one-in three." On
the other hand, from the standpoint of our experience of God, the
trinitarian framework is important. In his book *Systematic
Theology*, Gordon Kaufman states that

> at every point God's presence in history involves his threefold-
> ness. The first person (Father) signifies God's transcendence of
> the historical process at each point and in its entirety; the second
> person (Son) refers to his special involvement in the person-
> event Jesus Christ—and this of course also means his involvement
> in the preceding particular history (Old Testament) leading up to
> and making possible the life of Jesus of Nazareth, as well as that
> succeeding particular history brought into being in and through
> his life, death, and resurrection (church history expanding into
> world history); the third person (Holy Spirit) designates his being
> in and with and under all events of history, his presence in every
> new present. God's being, as apprehended in Christian faith,
> cannot be conceived apart from this oneness in three-ness and
> three-ness in oneness.[1]

Thus we can speak of the doctrine of the Trinity as having functional value for us.

If we think in terms of our personal relationship to God, the three aspects of God as expressed in the Trinity commend themselves. We relate to God as our authority, one who has dominion over us, who deserves our respect, trust, and praise. The concept of "Father" upholds this aspect of God. But our knowledge of God cannot remain transcendent and distant from us, and thus vague and undefined. We benefit by a knowledge of God that is concrete and focused in space and time. This is afforded us in the Son, Jesus Christ, as God's self-manifestation. Finally, we understand God not only as authoritative and transcendent (Father) and as distant and focused (Jesus), but as active and present here and now in a continuing way throughout life (the Holy Spirit). Thus our knowledge of God has these three necessary dimensions.

In Conclusion

God's revelation to us has sometimes been compared to the way in which we come to know a friend. Upon first acquaintance we learn some things about a person. As the relationship grows, our knowledge and awareness increase. However, there is no point at which we know everything about our friend. Each conversation and each new experience shows us yet another dimension of the person. Even humanly speaking, we can never say, "Now I know you fully."

Our knowledge of God is gained in a similar way—through God's Word and actions, and in a life of relationship with Him. God has chosen the boundaries of history—from the beginning of the world to the end—to make himself known to us. In our little lifetime we are afforded a glimpse of His character. While it is only a glimpse, it is sufficient for time and eternity.

TOPICS FOR DISCUSSION
1. Ways in which God reveals himself to us.
2. Modes of revelation reported in the Scriptures.
3. Obstacles to our knowledge of God; personal, societal, cultural.
4. The importance of the doctrine of the Trinity.
5. Ascertaining the word of God through the following: Scripture, the community of faith, conscience, world events, prayer, parental advice, church history, the Holy Spirit.

SELECTED SCRIPTURE PASSAGES
John 1:1-18
1 John 1:5—2:11
Psalm 121
Exodus 20

AIDS TO REFLECTION
"He comes to us as One unknown, without a name, as of old, by the lake-side, He came to those men who knew Him not. He speaks to us the same word: 'Follow thou me!' and sets us to the tasks which He has to fulfil for our time. He commands. And to those who obey Him, whether they be wise or simple, He will reveal Himself in the toils, the conflicts, the sufferings which they shall pass through in His fellowship, and, as an ineffable mystery, they shall learn in their own experience Who He is." Albert Schweitzer, *The Quest of the Historical Jesus* (New York: The Macmillan Company, 1961), p. 403.

"While in the past we were often content to let divine transcendence signify God's independent existence above human history, contemporary theologians prefer to think of divine transcendence as signifying the mode of God's immanence. The doctrine of divine transcendence specifies the manner in which God is present to life and history. God's presence is never identical with history or any moment of it; God's presence never absorbs it or is limited by it; the divine presence remains forever a summons to change history, an orientation to move it toward a more human future, a judgment on present sin, and a promise for ultimate victory." Gregory Baum, *New Horizons* (New York: Paulist Press, 1972), p. 81.

FOR FURTHER READING
Leon Morris, *I Believe in Revelation*. Grand Rapids: Eerdmans, 1976.
Henry Poettcker and Rudy Regehr, eds., *Call to Faithfulness: Essays in Canadian Mennonite Studies*. Winnipeg: Canadian Mennonite Bible College, 1972. See especially the first five essays.
David Schroeder, *Learning to Know the Bible*. Newton, Kans.: Faith and Life Press, 1966.

4/CREATION

When thou sendest forth thy Spirit, they are created; and thou renewest the face of the ground. Psalm 104:30

The Biblical View

The origin of the universe has proved to be a troublesome problem among Christians. Many scientific explorations and discoveries seek to shed light on such questions as these: When did the universe come into being? How old is the earth? How did the world come into existence? Is there an evolutionary relationship between man and the animals? Many discussions have been held on the question of whether the biblical view of creation, as reflected in Genesis 1 and 2, makes sense in the light of scientific discoveries. Some have upheld science against the Bible, while others have argued for the biblical position and against the scientific view.

It must be admitted that there have been mistakes on both sides of the argument. While scientific research needs to be taken seriously, scientific data has sometimes been treated as though it can supply final answers to final questions. We need to see that even the scientist works with theories, with *possible* explanations of things. Research is guided by its own viewpoint. Among Bible believers the first chapter of Genesis has sometimes been treated as though it were a scientific textbook, able to supply the bare facts needed for a modern-day scientific view. This also gets us into difficulty. The account of creation in Genesis is written against the background of the questions of Old Testament biblical times, and not as direct answers to present-day scientific questions.

Scientific exploration into the created universe can be a very exciting venture, but we must be cautious about the conclusions we draw from such explorations. It's one thing to calculate the distance between the earth and the sun, to determine what kinds of gases burn on the sun, or to plot the sun's course. It would be saying too much, however, to claim that such knowledge gives us power over the sun—the power to call the sun into being, to direct its course, and to guide its way to a meaningful end. In dealing with such ultimate questions we find ourselves in the area of faith. It is on this deeper level that the biblical view of creation is instructive for us. What are the important teachings about creation that we can draw from the Scriptures?

Creation by God

"In the beginning God created the heavens and the earth" (Gen.

1:1). This is a statement of faith. It is not possible to prove this statement with hard evidence. To be sure, Scripture makes this affirmation, but we must hasten to add that the scriptural account as we have it in Genesis 1 and 2 is also in the form of an invitation to *believe* that the Lord God, the Father of the people of Israel, of Jesus, and of the Christian church, is the Maker of heaven and earth.

In Israel's time, when the biblical account of creation was being written down and received, other claims were also being made as explanations for the created world. Creation stories can be found in Mesopotamia, in Egypt, in Africa, in Central America, and in other places. Space does not permit us to make a comparative study of the various accounts of creation here. Suffice it to say that the biblical account of creation, in specific aspects and taken as a whole, constitutes an invitation to "choose this day whom you will serve" (Josh. 24:15). Primarily, the Bible speaks to the question of *who* created the heavens and the earth, and invites us to believe that the Lord God is the Creator.

> Have you not known? Have you not heard?
> Has it not been told you from the beginning?
> Have you not understood from the foundations of the earth?
> It is he who sits above the circle of the earth,
> and its inhabitants are like grasshoppers;
> who stretches out the heavens like a curtain,
> and spreads them like a tent to dwell in;
> who brings princes to nought,
> and makes the rulers of the earth as nothing. . . .
>
> Have you not known? Have you not heard?
> The Lord is the everlasting God,
> the Creator of the ends of the earth.
>
> (Is. 40:21-23, 28)

What is said about creation in the Bible does not stand by itself. Rather, creation is understood in the light of the covenant and within salvation history. The account of creation carries with it the promise from God that He is working in the world to fulfill His purpose for mankind. The account of creation is in effect an invitation to trust that "God has the whole world in His hands," and to sense our responsibility to God as we work and play in the created world. To believe that God created the world leads us to receive all that is within the world as a gift from the Creator, and to cultivate a holy respect for our surroundings.

Order out of Chaos

"The earth was without form and void, and darkness was upon the face of the deep; and the Spirit of God was moving over the face of the waters" (Gen. 1:2).

In an ancient Babylonian creation epic, *Enuma Elish*, the story goes that the creation of the world arose out of a conflict between Marduk, the god of order, and Tiamat, the goddess of chaos. Marduk was victorious in the battle and hewed the fish-like body of Tiamat in pieces. The pieces of the body of Tiamat were then used as material in the creation of the universe. In the Bible one can still find passages which remind us of this Babylonian myth. The phrase "without form and void" in the above passage reminds us of the idea of chaos. Also, the word for *deep* in the Hebrew is *telom*, a word closely related to the name Tiamat, the goddess of chaos.

In contrast to the Babylonian epic, however, the Scriptures emphasize an important point. The creation of the world does not arise out of conflict. It is not a matter of God entering into dramatic battle in which the outcome is not at all assured, where the results are left to the fateful outcome of a skirmish or to a cunning power struggle. If this were the case, we would have to think of our lives as determined, day by day, by the successes and defeats enjoyed and suffered by the power struggle of the gods in the heavens. There would be no basis for a deep hope in God. Rather, according to Genesis, creation occurred through the consciously planned purposive will of God. He stood above chaos, and from that vantage point He proceeded to put things in their place. He was not a part of the "darkness" and the "deep." He stood "over" the situation and spoke His creative word into its midst. This is emphasized further in Genesis 1:3-5—"And God said, 'Let there be light'; and there was light. . . . And God separated the light from the darkness. . . . And there was evening and there was morning, one day." Indeed, the entire first chapter of Genesis portrays creation as orderly and purposeful, as the methodical work of the Creator.

Practically, this means that we can trust God not to let us down. It was not His intention to make this world chaotic or to make our personal lives meaningless. He is ready and willing to surround us and to infuse us with order and purpose. This is not always obvious, for we are the products of a long civilization that has sinned against God by working against His will and purpose. Yet even in the face of this, it is possible through faith and commitment to trust in the goodness of the Creator.

> For thus says the Lord, who created the heavens (he is God!),
> who formed the earth and made it (he established it;
> he did not create it a chaos, he formed it to be inhabited):
> "I am the Lord, and there is no other.
>
> I did not speak in secret, in a land of darkness;
> I did not say to the offspring of Jacob, 'Seek me in chaos.'
> I the Lord speak the truth, I declare what is right" (Is. 45:18, 19).

Creation Is Good

In the first chapter of Genesis the words "And God saw that it was good" occur five times (verses 10, 12, 18, 21, 25). In the last verse of the chapter we read, "And God saw everything that he had made, and behold, it was very good" (verse 31). In the second chapter of Genesis we find the idea of the goodness of creation again. The trees in the garden are said to be "pleasant to the sight and good for food" (Gen. 2:9). The creation of woman as a mate for man is a "good" thing. The Lord God observed that man was alone, and said, "It is not good that the man should be alone; I will make him a helper fit for him" (Gen. 2:18). Thereupon woman was created, thus making the situation "good."

The meaning of the little word *good* gives us a clue as to how we are to view the created universe and all that is in it. To say that creation is good is to emphasize that it is suited for a purpose; it has been prepared for a goal. That is, creation is good for its intended purpose. God has a goal for the universe. He has a history in mind for His created order. He will bring the created order to its intended goal.

That does not mean that everything done on the earth is always good. It is possible for the created world, especially man, to contribute to evil purposes. This is contrary to the deepest longing of the created order and can upset the ongoing plan of creation for a time. But despite these negative experiences, God is the Lord of creation. In time He will realize His good goal.

The lesson in this for us is that we are invited to think positively of the created world. We are free to enjoy its resources and its beauty. This includes the world of insects, of plants, of fishes, and of animals. This also includes the world of people as individuals and as societies. At the same time, there is a decision to be made. As we relate to the created world, will we seek to know God's good purpose for it, or will we use and abuse people and things toward ends that prove to be destructive and evil?

The emphasis upon the goodness of creation also carries a double-sided note of joy. God enjoys His work as Creator; and mankind is invited to find joy in it as well. That God has found joy in His creation is hinted at when we note the great variety of created things: beautiful plants, fruitful trees, peculiar sea animals, tiny insects that can only be seen through a microscope, heavenly bodies that can only be viewed through a telescope, countless varieties of birds and animals. The joy of His creative work is also evident in His creation of persons.

The created universe is "good" when it brings joy to us. God created things for our enjoyment. Yet such enjoyment cannot be haphazard or irresponsible. Joy comes when we live with attitudes of love and care for our surroundings. Our enjoyment of creation cannot be selfish. It must be shared enjoyment.

New Creation

The act of creation is not a one-time event in the misty past. Creation is happening every day of our lives. On one level, the changes occurring in the universe as the earth and other heavenly bodies move from stage to stage are affected by the creative work of God. On a more personal level, the positive changes that occur in individuals and in society belong to the creative power of God. The Scriptures teach us to pray, "Create in me a clean heart, O God" (Ps. 51:10). Persons who have discovered a relationship with Christ are described as "a new creation" (2 Cor. 5:17). Thus, the creative activity of God continues among us.

We can go one step further. The work of creation presses on toward a future expectation. It is the promise of Scripture that a time will come when the original purpose of God expressed in the perfect world of Genesis 1 will arrive. At present, "the creation waits with eager longing . . . because the creation itself will be set free from its bondage to decay and obtain the glorious liberty of the children of God" (Rom. 8:19, 21). This means that at some future time the sin of the world which hinders the creative work of God will be finally removed. In that day the order and peace of the first week of creation will become permanent. In its last pages the Bible envisions "a new heaven and a new earth" (Rev. 21:1) in which God will "make all things new" (21:5). In our day we see footprints and signs of the Creator's work. This gives us the hope that the Creator will fulfill His promise.

TOPICS FOR DISCUSSION
1. What Genesis 1 and 2 teach us about the Creator and creation.
2. Creation as an ongoing event.
3. Jesus Christ as the new "Creator."
4. Present-day participation in the work of the Creator.
5. God and mankind mutually responsible for creation.

SELECTED SCRIPTURE PASSAGES
Genesis 1
Isaiah 45:18, 19
Psalm 145:4-7, 10-16
Malachi 2:10
Romans 8:18-25
Psalm 104

AIDS TO REFLECTION
"The purpose and therefore the meaning of creation is to make possible the history of God's covenant with man which has its beginning, its centre and its culmination in Jesus Christ. The history of this covenant is as much the goal of creation as creation itself is the beginning of this history." Karl Barth, *Church Dogmatics*, vol. III, part 1 (Edinburgh: T. & T. Clark, 1958), p. 42.

"It is quite natural . . . that Christian devotion and Christian thought should concern themselves most with God's redeeming activity in Jesus Christ. . . . Nevertheless, the centrality of God's redeeming activity to our life and thought should not blind Christians to the divine work of creation, which, if not so close to our hearts, is just as significant for our existence and just as important if we are to think rightly about God." Langdon Gilkey, *Maker of Heaven and Earth* (Garden City: Doubleday & Company, Inc., 1965), p. 83.

"When you understand all about the sun and all about the atmosphere and all about the rotation of the earth, you may still miss the radiance of the sunset." Alfred North Whitehead, *Science and the Modern World* (New York: The Macmillan Company, 1926), p. 286.

"A full appreciation of not only the beauty but of the holiness of the Earth and of the immense creative investment that has gone into producing it, including as an integral component man himself, is essential to man's continued occupation of this planet. . . . To do this it is first necessary for man widely and generally to recover his lost sense of transcendent reality." William G. Pollard, "The Uniqueness of the Earth," in Ian G. Barbour, *Earth Might Be Fair* (Englewood Cliffs, New Jersey: Prentice-Hall, Inc., 1972), pp. 96f.

FOR FURTHER READING

Claus Westermann, *Creation*. Philadelphia: Fortress Press, 1974.

Gordon Kaufman, *Systematic Theology*. New York: Charles Scribner's Sons, 1968. Chapters 18 to 22.

John Reumann, *Creation and New Creation*. Minneapolis: Augsburg Publishing House, 1973.

5/MAN

Then the Lord God formed man of dust from the ground, and breathed into his nostrils the breath of life; and man became a living being.
Genesis 2:7

Who am I? What value do I place upon myself? What do my friends and relatives think of me? How can I know whether or not I have worth?

We have some simple and some sophisticated ways of answering these questions. A simple word of praise sometimes causes us to walk very tall, whereas a mild put-down depresses us into oblivion. On the sophisticated side, there are the scientists who calculate our worth in terms of chemical components, the economists who measure us in terms of our annual salary, the evolutionists who see us as one with the apes, or the humanists who claim that man is some kind of god.

People who touch our lives are constantly giving us impressions of what they think of us. The total picture they paint is probably somewhat blurry—shaded with acceptance and rejection, goodness and badness, optimism and pessimism. After all is said, it is sometimes difficult to know what to believe and what to take "with a grain of salt." We form our own opinion of how we will view ourselves partly on the basis of what others think and partly on personal convictions.

A certain amount of this is good. However, we can get carried away with our own ideas to the point where they become false notions of who we really are. While the opinions of others as well as our own ideas are helpful in telling us who we are, Christians gain a framework for their self-definition from the Bible. How is the question of the estimate of man answered in the Scriptures?

Not Too High

Every person experiences the temptation now and then in life to claim more than is possible. The young person who feels the freedom to be able to make her own decisions takes this feeling a step too far when she says, "I can do anything I want!" The man who becomes obsessed with personal accomplishments oversteps his limits when he thinks to himself, "I'm the greatest! I've reached the top! I have only myself to thank for this!" When a person believes this to the extent that it shapes personal faith, then God is no longer given His rightful place as the Creator. Rather, man has been tempted to take God's place.

From the very first pages onward, the Bible states that man is one of the creatures created by the Lord God. The first chapter of the

Bible begins with the words "In the beginning God created. . ." (Gen. 1:1). Later in the same chapter we read, "Then God said, 'Let us make man. . .'" (Gen. 1:26). In the second chapter of Genesis we read, "Then the Lord God formed man of dust from the ground, and breathed into his nostrils the breath of life; and man became a living being" (Gen. 2:7). We are not self-sufficient beings, but are dependent upon our Creator.

The biblical understanding of man wants to ensure that we do not overstep our human boundaries. Man is made to fit into a scheme which the Lord has designed. We do not have limitless powers to do whatever we want. That possibility belongs only to God the Creator. Psalm 100:3 expresses our place in the divine order of things: "Know that the Lord is God! It is he that made us, and we are his; we are his people, and the sheep of his pasture."

Practically, the emphasis upon man's creatureliness over against the Creator's sovereignty inspires an attitude of praise and humility in us. We are invited to praise God rather than ourselves as the source from which life flows. We receive the gift of life with humility and thanksgiving.

Not Too Low

At the same time, we must not overemphasize the submissive and creaturely aspect of man. In the biblical view there is another side to the coin. Man is wonderfully made. The psalmist says, ". . . Thou hast made him little less than God, and dost crown him with glory and honor" (Ps. 8:5). Genesis 1:27 states somewhat enthusiastically that "God created man in his own image, in the image of God he created him." This means, as the noted Old Testament theologian Eichrodt has said, that as human beings we have a share in the personhood of God. The character of God is reflected in the nature of man.

Theologians have sometimes tried to relate the image of God in man to some element of human equipment such as the mind or the conscience. But this is not what is meant. Rather, the image of God is reflected in the entire person. It is a way of expressing the fact that man has a special relationship to God as compared to the rest of creation. Man is capable of self-awareness and of self-determination. Furthermore, man is capable of responsible conduct. Above all, made in God's image, man is able to experience personal contact with God, and thus to respond creatively to the divine word. This involves man's total being, not just a part of him.

Along with being created in the image of God, man is given "dominion" (Gen. 1:26, 28) over the earth and all things in it. This means that man is told to care for the earth that God has created. We are to be "the gardeners of God." We are capable of this because we are endowed with the image of God. Thus we are invited to be creative workers, continuing the creative work which the Lord has originated.

The task implied here is quite serious. It involves taking responsibility for the earth in a way that continues the visions and goals that the Creator had in mind in the first place. It means dealing responsibly with every aspect of the earth—with all the things that surround us in life. To deal responsibly with the earth means to use all things for the praise of God and in service to fellow human beings.

Male and Female

One of the obvious facts of life is the existence of two kinds of persons: male and female. The biblical text on creation includes references to this fact. In Genesis 1:27 we read, "Male and female he created them." The second chapter of Genesis states that "the Lord God formed man of dust from the ground, and breathed into his nostrils the breath of life" (2:7). Further, the chapter contains a depiction of how the Lord God took one of Adam's ribs and made it into a woman (see 2:18-23).

What do these passages teach us? To be male and female is a part of God's work of creation. Thus it is a good thing. Consequently, we can accept the differentiation and relationship between the sexes as a part of God's good plan for us.

Freedom Within Limits

As a person grows from infancy into childhood, it soon becomes apparent that if one wants to live in this world, there are certain boundaries which need to be respected. If you place your hand on the hot element of a stove, it will burn. If you walk too close to the edge of the cliff, you will fall over the edge. At the same time, not all of life spells "limited." There are countless opportunities to relate positively to people and things, and to grow in these relationships.

The fact that life is filled with both limitless and limiting aspects is depicted in Genesis 2:8-17. The Lord God prepares a luscious garden into which He puts man (2:8). The garden has an abundance of trees that appeal to man's aesthetic hunger (trees that are "pleasant to the sight," 2:9) and that meet his physical needs (trees that are "good for food," 2:9). These two kinds of trees represent the kind of world every person is born into even today. All around us the world offers satisfactions in terms of the hunger for beauty and for food. Our needs in these areas are met through the resources of the earth, both natural and manufactured. The beautiful and productive "trees" mentioned in Genesis 2:9 are representative of the richness of God's created world inasmuch as it satisfies our needs. Enjoy the earth and all that is in it!

But wait! There is at least one tree that is off-limits—"Of the tree of the knowledge of good and evil you shall not eat, for in the day that you eat of it you shall die" (Gen. 2:17). The presence of "the tree of the knowledge of good and evil" in the midst of the many other trees represents a warning to us as we enjoy God's good earth. The tree reminds us that we are man and not God. We are creatures and not the Creator. Specifically, to eat of the tree represents the temptation to put ourselves above God by assuming that man, rather than God, is the source of knowledge. It is the act of trying to put God aside and pretend that we are God.

This is never successful, since we were fashioned as man and not as God. We were made so as to receive knowledge from God but not to become the source of it. To attempt to "play God" can only lead to self-destruction: "For in the day that you eat of it you shall die" (Gen. 2:17). The point is that it is possible for man to obtain knowledge from God provided he is ready to receive it as a gift of God's goodness and not as an achievement for which man himself takes the credit. Man was, and is still, created in such a way as to find true fulfillment only by submitting to God's scheme of things and working creatively within this order.

A second special tree is referred to as well—the tree of life (Gen. 2:9; 3:22, 24). As with the tree of knowledge, this tree also represents a special gift which God desires for man—the gift of eternal life. The danger is there, however, that man will seek to attain eternal life in his own strength without recognizing the eternal Lord God as the Giver of life. Eventually man is driven from the Garden of Eden lest after having eaten of the tree of knowledge, "he put forth his hand and take also of the tree of life, and eat, and live for ever" (3:22). The Lord desires to endow man with eternal life, but this must be received as a gift in God's own time and must not be attempted as a self-styled achievement by man in his own strength. Lest man attempt something so foolhardy, he is driven from the beautiful garden and surrounded in part by "thorns and thistles" which should be a constant reminder of the limitations of earthly existence.

This is our lot as we experience life from day to day. While a glimpse of Eden still remains on our earth in that there is beauty all around us and we have food, shelter, and clothing, we are also quite immersed in a world of sweat, toil, and inevitable death. These elements remind us that we are creatures and not Creators.

Hope for the Future

Because of the Fall of man, the image of God in us has been tarnished. While there is some good in what we are and do, mankind is not a perfect reflection of the personhood of God. Our earth is not the Garden of Eden. Where does this leave us? The coming of Jesus Christ to earth brought with it the opportunity for man to reestablish fellowship with the Father. His words and deeds gave us clues as to how the kingdom of God could be expressed in part upon earth. Furthermore, His death and resurrection carry the promise of a future restoraton of a heavenly Eden in which the goals that the Creator had in mind for first man will be realized. In that day we will attain "to the measure of the stature of the fulness of Christ" (Eph. 4:13).

In the meantime the Christian faith teaches us to be quite realistic about ourselves. We cannot expect to attain to the stature of God here on earth. Nor should we degrade ourselves, thinking we are of no worth. We should live "in the middle" between these two extremes.

TOPICS FOR DISCUSSION
1. The biblical view of persons as having potential for good and for evil.
2. The uniqueness of a self-definition that is based upon a relationship with God.
3. How Jesus Christ viewed persons.

4. Living between limitation and freedom.
5. How we view, and how we are viewed by, ourselves; our acquaintances; our church; our parents; our teachers.

SELECTED SCRIPTURE PASSAGES
Job 14
Psalm 8
Colossians 3:5-17
Genesis 1:26-31
Genesis 2:4-9, 15-25

AIDS TO REFLECTION
"Man is a profound riddle to himself, for he bears witness to the existence of a higher world. The superhuman principle is a constituent element of man's nature. Man is discontented with himself and capable of outgrowing himself. The very fact of the existence of man is a break in the natural world and proves that nature cannot be self-sufficient but rests upon a supernatural reality." Nicolas Berdyaev, *The Destiny of Man* (New York: Harper & Row, 1960), pp. 45f.

"This fragile life between birth and death can nevertheless be a fulfillment—if it is a dialogue." Martin Buber, *Man to Man* (London & Glasgow: Collins, 1947).

"If man would believe that the historical context into which he has been thrown were meaningful, if he could believe it to be the expression of the loving personal decision and purpose of a compassionate Father who is moving all history toward a significant goal, then anxiety would be dissolved. If he could believe his existence and decisons and actions had an indispensable place within larger purposes shaping the overall movement of history, and that even his stupid blunders and wilful perversities could be rectified and redeemed, his anxiousness and guilt could give place to confidence, creativeness, hope. This, of course, is precisely the claim of the Christian Gospel: the overall movement of cosmic history is in the hands of the God and Father of Jesus Christ. God loves man, God gives himself to man in Jesus Christ, God continuously seeks to bring man into his community of love and freedom and creativity." Gordon Kaufman, *Systematic Theology* (New York: Charles Scribner's Sons, 1968), p. 350.

FOR FURTHER READING

Wolfhart Pannenberg, *What Is Man?* Philadelphia: Fortress Press, 1970.

Carl E. and LaVonne Braaten, *The Living Temple: A Practical Theology of the Body and the Foods of the Earth.* New York: Harper & Row, 1976.

Reinhold Niebuhr, *The Nature and Destiny of Man.* 2 vols. New York: Charles Scribner's Sons, 1943.

6/SIN

"Father, I have sinned against heaven and before you; I am no longer worthy to be called your son." Luke 15:21

According to the first two chapters of the Bible, man was created good. However, we should not think of his goodness as a stable and fixed state. He was also created as a human person. This means that he was equipped with the freedom to make decisions. He could decide for or against the Creator's plan for his life. Thus from the very beginning man was created with the potentiality for good or for evil. He had the power to build positively on what God had set in motion in the original act of creation, or he could work destructively against God's plan.

The question is sometimes asked, Why did God allow the possibility of disobedience and sin? Why did He not create man in such a way that the initial goodness would be preserved for time and eternity? To think in this way is to misunderstand God. God is not a puppeteer who needs only to pull the strings to make us do his bidding. There are religions that understand God's relation to man in this way. They think that the course of man has been fixed in all its details from birth, and that it is only a matter of discovering the mysterious plan that God has programmed for every person.

While the Christian faith believes in a God who has a plan for our lives, it is wrong to think in terms of a necessary and fixed scheme. We were created as free beings. God desires that we live in His will, but He will not force us. He wants us to want to respond to His love. Our faith places great value on a cooperative working relationship between God and man. Man is seen as a contributing partner in God's work in the world, including the shaping of the historical process. It is because of God's desire for man's positive cooperation that the possibility of rebellion is there.

The Fall

The trees in the Garden of Eden symbolize the somewhat precarious freedom of man. On the one hand, he is invited to follow the will of God by enjoying the beautiful and productive trees in the garden. That is, man is free to explore and to enjoy the earth and all that is in it. On the other hand, the tree of the knowledge of good and evil symbolizes the warning that man must not misuse his freedom. The tree stands as a caution against the temptation to "be like God" (Gen. 3:5). It is significant that the very gift with which man has been endowed by God—freedom which makes man able to be creative—is sometimes used by man to turn against God.

To try to "be like God" is, in the final analysis, our greatest temptation. All sin can be put under this one umbrella. To eat of the tree of knowledge is, in effect, to push God out of our lives—to claim that we are masters of our own destiny, that we are self-made individuals, that no one else can tell us what is good for us. In doing so we seek to deny the most fundamental truth about our existence, namely, that God is our Creator and our Sustainer.

Adam and Eve did what we too would have done, had we been in the Garden of Eden. They yielded to the temptation of the serpent: "You will not die. For God knows that when you eat of it your eyes will be opened, and you will be like God, knowing good and evil" (Gen. 3:4, 5). They really believed that they could pull themselves up to a heavenly status by their own efforts. We would have yielded to the very same temptation as Adam and Eve did, because we have followed their thinking as well. It is very tempting to come up with our own self-styled solutions to life's great questions, or to discover a secret formula that will open our eyes to all mysteries, or to reach for something that appeals to our desires, but is dangerous. Furthermore, when we get caught, we react just as Adam did when he blamed Eve for his actions (Gen. 3:12: "The man said, 'The woman whom thou gavest to be with me, she gave me fruit of the tree, and I ate.'"). It is characteristic of man to offer excuses for actions when they become embarrassing. We do not readily confess that we are sinners. Rather, we try to hide the fact.

When the Lord saw what Adam and Eve had done, He drove them from the garden and gave them specific reminders of their downfall. For example, a woman will have pain in childbearing (Gen. 3:16); the ground will bring forth thorns and thistles (3:18); a man will experience toil (3:17) and sweat (3:19); death will overtake everyone (3:19). These are to be understood as signs and warnings of the fact that man cannot "be like God." He finds his true self only as the servant of God his Creator. He is not capable of mastering his own existence successfully for any length of time.

Are We Included?

Was the Fall only a problem for Adam and Eve? Have we learned our lesson from them? Or is every person a victim of temptation and sin?

In the remainder of the Old Testament and in the New Testament we find two answers to this question. On the one hand, there are many stories of persons who are unfaithful to the Lord. The list includes Cain, the people of Noah's day, the people who built the tower of Babel, Israel in the wilderness, King David, the people of Isaiah's time, and many others. The overwhelming grip of sin upon mankind is expressed by the psalmist in the words "Behold, I was brought forth in iniquity, and in sin did my mother conceive me" (Ps. 51:5). The psalmist concludes that because sin is so basic to man, we must have been born in sin. When the New Testament takes stock of man's condition, the conclusion is that "sin came into the world through one man" (Rom. 5:12), that "in Adam all die" (1 Cor. 15:22). Thus, "One man's trespass led to condemnation for all men" (Rom. 5:18). The Bible concludes that the Fall extends beyond Adam and Eve to include everyone: "All have sinned and fall short of the glory of God" (Rom. 3:23).

On the other hand, the Bible also tells of persons who have been faithful to the Lord at times in their life. The list includes Noah, Abraham, Isaac, Jacob, Joseph, Moses, and others in the Old Testament. In the New Testament we read of such figures as the disciple John, Mary and Martha, Stephen, Paul, and many others. It is not that these persons were perfect at all times. But they are recognized as examples of true faith in God and obedience to His will. The eleventh chapter of Hebrews supplies a list of persons who have shown outstanding faith in their day. The sixth and seventh chapters of the Book of Revelation tell of a multitude of saints who will be recognized as having been "servants of our God" (Rev. 7:3) in their lifetime. Thus, the Bible reports that man is still capable of responding to the Lord in obedience.

If we put these two answers to the question of our part in the Fall together, our conclusion would be somewhat as follows. The story of Adam and Eve is the story of everyone. Everyone receives life from the hand of the Creator as Adam and Eve did; everyone is born with a measure of freedom to take a chosen course; everyone is to be encouraged to live life to the full, but in such a way that the Creator is glorified, and not man. Further, it is evident that sin has pervaded the human race; everyone is infected in one way or another; everyone is tempted to question God's teachings and to attempt to be like God rather than accepting our status as children of God. And yet this infection is not total in the sense that we would be deprived completely of any good acts or intentions. Alongside of the evil in us, there is "a streak of good." In a later chapter we will relate the good and the evil in man to the work of Jesus Christ.

Two Viewpoints on Sin

In the history of the Christian church two classical positions have been taken on the theme of sin. One view sees sin as a state in which man is born. Because man is in this state, various unethical and immoral actions are committed by him. We sin because we are sinners by nature, and therefore we cannot do otherwise. St. Augustine formulated this position very early in the history of the church. Luther, Calvin, and Wesley also defended this view of "total depravity." Among the contemporary theologians who hold a similar view are Karl Barth and Reinhold Niebuhr.

A second view begins at a different point. Pelagius, who opposed the view of Augustine, argued that while Adam set a bad example for the human race, his fall ruined only himself. Later generations thus remain free to choose to do good! While Augustine would have said that man sins because he is a sinner, Pelagius would say that if man is a sinner, it is because he sins. We are sinners because we do wrong, not because we were born evil. Thus, according to Pelagius and a long line of theologians after him, sin is not connected with an inherited nature in man, but with individual acts which are done by persons in their lifetime.

In both history and present-day teaching of the Mennonite church one can identify both viewpoints. There are some ministers and teachers who emphasize original sin quite strongly, while others tend to speak of man as capable of goodness by nature, and of sins as the consequence of personal disobedience rather than something inherited at birth. Because of the emphasis upon "good works" in Mennonite theology, the second view sometimes comes to the fore.

The best solution is to seek for a balance between the two views. The Scriptures define sin as a consequence of the very nature of man. In Psalm 51:5 we read, "Behold, I was brought forth in iniquity, and in sin did my mother conceive me." But in numerous texts, sinfulness is also a consequence of wrong acts (for example, Isaiah 1:4). Thus in dealing with the problem of sin we contend with our very nature and also with our evil deeds. It is a matter of allowing the grace and power of Jesus Christ to meet us both at the point of our actions and our nature.

Dealing with Sin

The Lord gave Adam and Eve a chance to make a new beginning after their disobedience. Things were somewhat different now, since the act had been committed. Nonetheless, man was not rejected by God. Fellowship was restored, with God taking the initiative. That God is a loving Father who is willing to embrace the sinner is clearly shown in the teachings of both Old and New Testaments. The message of the prophet Isaiah to the rebellious people is evidence enough: "Come now, let us reason together, says the Lord: though your sins are like scarlet, they shall be as white as snow; though they are red like crimson, they shall become like wool" (Is. 1:18). The act of forgiveness is expressed supremely in Jesus Christ's death on the cross.

But forgiveness is often linked with a word of discipline. Sometimes this occurs in the form of punishment, as in the case of Adam and Eve. At other times the word of discipline constitutes a call to holy living. The words from Isaiah, quoted above, are followed by a condition: "If you are willing and obedient, you shall eat the good of the land; But if you refuse and rebel, you shall be devoured by the sword. . ." (1:19, 20). On one occasion Jesus forgave a person, and then added, "Go, and do not sin again" (Jn. 8:11). Thus, while forgiveness flows from the divine heart of grace, it is not to be assumed that grace can be accepted at a cheap price. To avoid making a farce of the grace of God, it is expected that the forgiven person will express thanksgiving through a life of discipleship.

One further matter needs to be mentioned. Christians are sometimes discouraged by the evil that is happening day by day in the world. There is often lovelessness among family members; our newspapers report endless cases of robbery and murder; on any given day there is warfare somewhere in the world. Add to this the endless catalogue of natural catastrophes such as hurricanes and earthquakes. What do we make of this? Is God really the Lord of the universe? Does He care?

This is a difficult problem. A few points can be offered as perspective for Christians. First, the Creator did not promise that the earth would be "a bed of roses." To some extent, at least, He has willed to let us try our hand at organizing life on earth, and much of the evil is our own doing. Secondly, the presence of evil pervades not only the life of man, but the intermediary spheres between heaven and earth as well. Evil has infected the foundations of the created order. Hence destructiveness is often evidenced in the natural world.

We have the promise that in His own time at the close of this age God will put all things under His feet, and will dispel the forces of Satan once and for all. Christians look forward in hope to that glorious day when sin will be no more. However, in the meantime we can do more than fold our hands and wait. It is the Christian's duty to introduce the reality of the coming kingdom here and now.

TOPICS FOR DISCUSSION

1. The rise of sin in the created order: its possibility because of freedom; its occurrence among the angels; its occurrence among first man; its continuation in history.
2. The difference and similarity between a sinful nature and a sinful act.
3. What Jesus Christ taught and did about sin.
4. Can one stop sinning, or is sin inevitable?
5. Ways of overcoming sin: the role of prayer; the importance of confession; the Christian community as a resource.
6. Scriptural guidance for dealing with sin.

SELECTED SCRIPTURE PASSAGES

Genesis 3
Psalm 51
Amos 8
Romans 6
Luke 15

AIDS TO REFLECTION

"In some form all of us repeat the experience of Adam and Eve in the Garden of Eden, seeking to eat of the Tree of the Knowledge of Good and Evil in order to find out for ourselves whether what has been told us is the real right and wrong of things." Karl Menninger, *Whatever Became of Sin?* (New York: Hawthorn Books, Inc., 1973), p. 20.

"What is the situation which is the occasion of temptation? Is it not the fact that man is a finite spirit, lacking identity with the whole, but yet a spirit capable in some sense of envisaging the whole, so that he easily commits the error of imagining himself the whole which he envisages?" Reinhold Niebuhr, *The Nature and Destiny of Man*, vol. I (New York: Charles Scribner's Sons, 1941), p. 181.

"He remembers our sin no more for ever, yet we remember it against ourselves; and indeed it is more than doubtful whether in any real sense a Christian can ever 'forgive himself' for wrong-doing. This settled sense of unworthiness is commonly more profound, though less emotionally piercing, in the old than the young. But whereas before reconciliation with God the feeling of guilt is purely disabling and suffuses the moral life with the consciousness of radical failure, later, as an undertone of felt unworthiness, it aids in fostering that humility and receptiveness apart from which the life of God cannot be ours." H. R. Mackintosh, *The Christian Experience of Forgiveness* (London & Glasgow: Collins Clear-Type Press, 1961), p. 71.

FOR FURTHER READING

Karl Menninger, *Whatever Became of Sin?* New York: Hawthorn Books, 1973.

Paul M. Miller, *The Devil Did Not Make Me Do It*. Scottdale, Pa.: Herald Press, 1977.

7/INCARNATION

No one has ever seen God; the only Son, who is in the bosom of the Father, he has made him known. John 1:18

Jesus Christ stands at the center of our Christian faith. To be a Christian means, primarily, to attach oneself to Jesus. Who is this Jesus? What did He do for us? We must begin our answer to this question by characterizing the main features of His earthly ministry. Thereafter we will deal with the question of His meaning for us (chapter 8).

His Birth

Almost two thousand years ago a baby was born in Bethlehem. He was announced by a host of angels and greeted by shepherds and wise men. What was so special about the baby Jesus?

First, there was the family background of His birth. He had an important heritage. While He was the son of Joseph and Mary, the Gospel of Matthew traces His lineage to Abraham, the patriarchal father of the Israelites (Mt. 1:1-16). The Gospel of Luke traces Jesus' heritage back even further to Adam (Lk. 3:23-38). Jesus was a son of the people of Israel as well as the Son of God.

Second, there were the special promises that accompanied the announcement of His birth. Mary was told that Jesus was to be called "the Son of the Most High" (Lk. 1:32); that He would be a successor to King David (1:32); that His kingdom would last forever (1:33); that He would restore the fortunes of the people of Israel (1:68-72); that He would give light to all peoples (2:32). In short, Jesus was the long-awaited Redeemer of the world.

His Baptism and Temptation

After a period of growth Jesus began His ministry. He left His home and presented himself to John the Baptist for baptism at the Jordan River. Jesus was baptized for several reasons: (1) It was an act of identification with the repentant people of Israel. That is, He declared himself to be a part of the great movement of God which begins with a preparation of the heart through repentance (see Mark 1:1-5). We believe that Jesus was not a sinner and thus did not require repentance. Yet in the act of baptism He showed us that He belongs to the same community with us. (2) The baptism was the occasion when God could declare and reveal to the people that Jesus was His special Son (Mt. 3:17; Mk. 1:11; Jn. 1:31). (3) The baptism serves as a commissioning service which began His ministry.

Following His baptism Jesus was tempted in the wilderness. The temptation of Jesus was a test of Jesus' devotion to His heavenly Father. The devil wanted Jesus to put God's promises to the test: Does God really expect You to live by His word (Mt. 4:3, 4)? Has God really promised that He will rescue You from all danger (4:5-7)? What is the use of worshiping God alone (4:8-10)? Would Jesus follow the directives of the devil, or would He remain true to God? In the end Jesus sent the devil away with these words: "You shall worship the Lord your God and him only shall you serve" (Mt. 4:10).

The temptation of Jesus reminds us of the temptation of Adam and Eve. They were also tempted to question their special relationship with God. Like Jesus, they were tempted to act in their own strength rather than rely on God. The only difference is that Jesus withstood temptation, while Adam and Eve did not. In Philippians 2:6, 7 we read, "Though he was in the form of God, (he) did not count equality with God a thing to be grasped, but emptied himself, taking the form of a servant. . . ." Unlike Jesus, Adam and Eve tried to make themselves equal with God. This was their downfall.

The Ministry of Jesus on Earth

The ministry of Jesus can be summarized in one line: "The kingdom of God is at hand" (Mk. 1:15). By this was meant that with the coming of Jesus Christ a new age was dawning upon earth. In one sense the new age was not new. Rather, it was a restoration of what God had originally intended when He created the heavens and the earth in the beginning. There should be perfect fellowship between God and man and between man and man. Furthermore, there should be no discrimination between the rich and poor, between Jew and Gentile, or between the proud and the humble. All have an equal share in the goodness of God. Jesus was setting the stage for the coming of this kind of kingdom; in fact, He was playing the first act.

The people of Jesus' day should not have found His message strange. Their writings (the Old Testament) contained many words of hope and promise of the kingdom of God. Inspired by God's word of promise, Abraham had hoped to find the promised land at the end of his journey (Gen. 12). Led by the quest for freedom, Moses and the people of Israel sought the promised land beyond the Red Sea and the wilderness. The prophets of Israel had even become quite specific with their visions of a new Messiah whose kingdom could include all nations (Is. 2:1-4; 9:6, 7). They spoke of the birth of a king, a new "David," who would treat every person with justice. Jesus was sent from His Father to incarnate these promises, to inaugurate the kingdom of God.

An interesting feature of Jesus' work was the calling and training of His disciples. It was not uncommon for an influential teacher of biblical times to gather a group of students around him for the purpose of imparting his teachings to an inner group which would, in turn, be responsible for preserving and spreading the master's teachings. Apparently Jesus had many hearers who gathered at one place or another to learn from Him. However, there was a core group of twelve disciples who remained with Him over a longer period of time. It was their duty to understand Jesus' teachings clearly so that if and when Jesus would leave the earth, they could carry on with His work. Toward the end of His ministry He prayed concerning His disciples: "Sanctify them in the truth. . . . As thou didst send me into the world, so I have sent them into the world" (Jn. 17:17, 18). As we know, not every disciple in Jesus' inner circle was faithful to Him. Yet certain of His followers provided an important link in the earliest work of the church following the death and resurrection of their Master.

Jesus taught the message of the kingdom of God through word. His speeches to the people varied in length and style. Sometimes He gave long discourses such as the Sermon on the Mount (Mt. 5-7). On such occasions His inner group of disciples gathered near Him while the crowds stood on the fringes of the circle and listened. Some would come and go as He taught. At times He would be found in the synagogue on the Sabbath day, reading the Scriptures or offering a comment in the discussion that followed the reading. Often He taught his followers and would-be followers as He walked from village to village along the dusty roads. The occasion for His teachings was sometimes provided by the spur of the moment. Always the burden of His message was that God is expressing His divine will at this moment in history; and Jesus is the bearer of this message from God.

Not only what Jesus said but what He did also conveyed His message. He healed the sick, restored sight to the blind, ate with tax collectors and sinners, stilled the storms, fed the hungry, and restored the dead to life. The point of these deeds was not to show that modern laws of science could be broken or to pose as a magician. Through His miracles Jesus provided signs of the kingdom of God. Furthermore, the miracles were meant to reassure the faithful that His Father is still the Lord of His created order. God can overcome sickness and blindness, famine, and poverty. He is Lord of the natural world. He also overcomes sin by forgiving the sinner and inviting persons to new life. The work of the kingdom extends from the deeply personal needs of the individual to the farthest corners of the vast universe. This was the message that Jesus brought.

Many people in Jesus' day found His message strange. Some expected an actual king as God's Messiah. In their eyes Jesus was an unlikely candidate. Some wanted Him to take sides with the religious scribes and Pharisees, but Jesus tended to prefer the company of sinners and tax collectors. Some thought He should address himself only to the people of Abraham, but Jesus offered salvation to all people. Day after day He surprised the people with the unexpected. Even His own disciples could not understand Him at times. Yet He persistently set about the task of proclaiming the will of God.

No one who came in contact with Jesus in His day could pass Him by. He confronted people through word and deed in such a way that He evoked a reaction. Hearing the same words, some loved Him while others hated Him; some accepted Him while others rejected Him. At the beginning of His ministry He came to His hometown of Nazareth where, after reading a Scripture passage from Isaiah 61:1, 2, He told the people that they would probably reject Him as a prophet in their midst. In the course of the exchange they were angered by His biting words, and drove Him out of His own town (Lk. 4:16-30). On another occasion early in His ministry He spoke words of forgiveness and healing to a paralytic. Thereupon the scribes accused Him of blasphemy, questioning His right to speak and act in the name of God (Mk. 2:7). The words and works of the kingdom of God were a comfort to some but a stumbling block to others. One way or another, He could not be ignored. Everyone had to reckon with Him. In John 7:43, 44, we read that "there was a division among the people over him. Some of them wanted to arrest him, but no one laid hands on him."

The Death of Jesus

While according to the Gospels of Matthew and Luke there was rejoicing over the fact that Jesus was the Messiah, the Son of God, not everyone was overjoyed. King Herod had plotted to do away with the infant Jesus because He was a threat to his throne. The aged Simeon who met Mary and Joseph with the babe in the temple blessed them with these words: "Behold, this child is set for the fall and rising of many in Israel, and for a sign that is spoken against..." (Lk. 2:34). It appeared from the very beginning that Jesus would be greeted by both positive and negative responses.

During the course of His ministry some believed and others doubted. The Gospel writer Mark depicted the story of Jesus' ministry as an unfolding drama in which Jesus gradually made himself known to the people. As He did so, there was growing tension. Eventually the disciples confessed, "You are the Christ" (Mk. 8:29). They recognized Jesus as the promised Messiah who saves His people from sin. At the same time, however, the Pharisees used every possible occasion to test Him. They believed that He was possessed by a demon rather than by the spirit of God. They finally became rigid in their view and sought His death.

In the face of this opposition, Jesus did not compromise His message in the least. Instead He impressed upon His disciples the difficulty of obedience: "If any man would come after me, let him deny himself and take up his cross and follow me. For whoever would save his life will lose it; and whoever loses his life for my sake and the gospel's will save it" (Mk. 8:34, 35). Furthermore, He spoke frequently of the inevitability of His own suffering and death: "Behold, we are going up to Jerusalem; and the Son of man will be delivered to the chief priests and the scribes, and they will . . . kill him..." (Mk. 10:33, 34). Jesus knew what would happen to Him if He continued to proclaim the message of God's kingdom without compromise.

The trial, conviction, and death took place in Jerusalem during the week of the celebration of the Jewish Passover. Early in the week Jesus had entered the temple and proceeded to drive out those who had made a business of the religious celebration. Later in the week He entered the city of Jerusalem riding upon a donkey. Both acts aroused the anger of the officials. The cleansing of the temple caught the attention of the religious and business community; the entry into Jerusalem was seen by the political leaders as a claim of kingship. Some religious government officials felt that these radical activities would cause trouble among the various factions in the land. Jesus had said again and again that He only wanted to call the people back to God's original purpose and that His kingdom was not of this world; yet, the leaders feared that especially during the week of the Passover when there were many visitors in the city, and when the hopes of the Jews for freedom from Roman rule were once more kindled, the presence of Jesus would only add fuel to the fire. Thus He was put to death on the cross as a political and religious radical.

The Resurrection and Ascension

The resurrection provided the grand finale to Jesus' life. The disciples were greatly discouraged by the death of their leader. But their mood changed when Jesus reappeared to them in a resurrected body. Now they knew that their faith had not been in vain. Jesus was truly the Son of God. Furthermore, they were assured that Jesus would be with them as a continuing spiritual presence in the future. When He ascended to heaven the disciples were told, "This Jesus, who was taken up from you into heaven, will come in the same way as you saw him go into heaven" (Acts 1:11). For the disciples it was now a matter of continuing the work which their Master had begun in anticipation of His eventual final return at the end of time.

TOPICS FOR DISCUSSION
1. The meaning of incarnation; the incarnation as a special miracle of God among us.
2. The significance of the temptation and baptism of Jesus.
3. The central features in the teachings of Jesus.
4. The significance of Jesus' acts of healing and other miracles for His message.
5. The cross: Could Jesus have done without it?
6. The sense in which Jesus is present in all of history and among us.

SELECTED SCRIPTURE PASSAGES
Isaiah 9:1-7
Isaiah 11:1-9
Isaiah 53
Luke 4:16-30

AIDS TO REFLECTION
"I think, therefore, that the purpose and the cause of the incarnation was that He might illuminate the world by His wisdom and excite it to the love of Himself." —Peter Abelard

"It is the experience of life that we have to live long with a person before we can know him in any real sense of the term. It is also the experience of life that the most valuable people in life are not the shallow people who carry all their goods in the shop window, but the people whose character and kindness, whose personality and wisdom grow more and more precious the longer we know them. This was necessarily the experience of the Christian Church and of the individual Christian in regard to Jesus Christ. The longer men think about Jesus the greater he becomes; and the longer they live with him the more they know that no human categories can contain him." William Barclay, *Crucified and Crowned* (London: SCM Press, 1961), p. 179.

"If a man came to you and said, 'I am the greatest preacher now living in the world,' how would you react to him? After a moment of astonishment you might well say, 'That is very nice for you; but how do you know, and how can you prove it?' There are many claims that we cannot accept merely because someone makes them. . . . Is not the position rather the same with regard to the claims of Jesus Christ? Even if He had said plainly, 'I am the Son of God,' we should still want proof. And what other proof could He offer than His words, His works, and His character?" Stephen Neill, *Who Is Jesus Christ?* (London: Lutterworth Press, 1956), p. 27.

FOR FURTHER READING
Archibald M. Hunter, *The Work and Words of Jesus.* London: SCM Press, 1950.

John Howard Yoder, *The Politics of Jesus.* Grand Rapids: Eerdmans, 1972.

Merrill C. Tenney, *The Reality of the Resurrection.* New York: Harper & Row, 1963.

For by grace you have been saved through faith; and this is not your own doing, it is the gift of God—not because of works, lest any man should boast. For we are his workmanship, created in Christ Jesus for good works, which God prepared beforehand, that we should walk in them. Ephesians 2:8-10

Among people who take Jesus Christ seriously, we find two typical attitudes toward Him: the attitude of admiration for what Christ did for us, and the attitude of obedience to Him. Ideally both are important, but there is the tendency to focus more upon one or the other. What Jesus did for us invites our admiration, our worship, and our confession of sin. In taking upon himself suffering and death, He did something for us that we cannot do for ourselves. Thus we say a hearty thank-you to Him. At the same time, we must not overemphasize this aspect of the good news. Jesus also did something for us that we are likewise called to do: He gave us "an example, that [we] should follow in his steps" (1 Pet. 2:21). Thus He invites our obedience as well. It is important that we not only fall down and worship Him, but also walk with Him in life.

The Setting for Salvation

In order to understand this two-sided aspect of the Son of God, we must refer to the first chapters of the Old Testament. In the beginning it was the will of God that man should live responsibly in the Garden of Eden. The garden provided abundant opportunities for life and growth, as is symbolized by "every tree that is pleasant to the sight and good for food" (Gen. 2:9). At the same time, there was a restriction, symbolized by "the tree of life" and "the tree of the knowledge of good and evil" (2:9). These trees point to the boundaries of life in man's relation to God. The two trees reminded the first man that God must always be seen as the Giver of life and as the Author of the law (what is "good" and what is "evil").

When Adam and Eve attempted to disregard this framework, thinking they could "be like God, knowing good and evil" (Gen. 3:5), they were driven from the garden. Henceforth Adam and Eve, together with their offspring, had a two-fold problem: First, how would it be possible for God to forgive man for the sin of disobedience? Second, how can man learn the way of God more clearly so that he can be prevented from repeating Adam's foolish mistake? For this problem a double-sided message was needed from God: a word of forgiveness for sin, and a word of direction for life.

We must never overlook the fact that the Old Testament already proclaimed this message of forgiveness and obedience in its own way. When Cain killed Abel, the Lord "put a mark on Cain, lest any who came upon him should kill him" (Gen. 4:15). The mark was a sign that the Lord had visited Cain with His word of forgiving grace. After the great Flood the Lord placed a rainbow in the sky as a sign of His promise "that never again shall all flesh be cut off by the waters of a flood, and never again shall there be a flood to destroy the earth" (9:11). The rainbow was a sign of the grace of God following a period of disobedience and punishment. The patriarchs (Abraham, Isaac, and Jacob) were given numerous directives from the Lord God which guided them in their pilgrimage of faith. The same can be said for Moses and the people of Israel. The Ten Commandments given at Sinai are a familiar example. Later, when the people of Israel settled in the land of Canaan, the prophets proclaimed their message of repentance and forgiveness to the unfaithful people. God was willing to forgive them if they would repent.

However, it must be said that persons in the time of the Old Testament found it difficult to understand the full meaning of the will of God. There was the knowledge that God is a forgiving God, but this was often overshadowed by an emphasis upon His harsh demands. While it was stated by priest and prophet that the Lord God visits His people with steadfast love and forgiveness, the message was not heard with sufficient clarity to make a lasting impact. And while Old Testament history displays a long tradition of rules and regulations, it is difficult to establish a clearly outlined directive for the life of the people. Furthermore, there was the constant danger that the people of Israel saw the word of the Lord as a word for the Israelites only, not for all mankind. This placed certain restrictions upon the universal will of God.

Thus it was not coincidental that the prophets looked forward to the birth of a Savior who would bring a light to people who walk in darkness (Is. 9:2). This special Son would exude "the spirit of wisdom and understanding, the spirit of counsel and might, the spirit of knowledge and the fear of the Lord" (Is. 11:2). He would bring a strong word from God both in terms of forgiveness and guidance. Preferably the word should be personal—in the form of an incarnate spokesman for the Lord. This personal word could provide the kind of impact that cannot be communicated adequately on tablets of stone or through traditional institutional structures such as the temple and the priesthood.

The Message of Jesus

Throughout the New Testament we find the two-sided emphasis upon Jesus as the One who forgave sins and as the One who provided an example for our life. This is already evident in the temptation of Jesus which occurred at the beginning of His ministry. Unlike Adam and Eve, Jesus withstood the subtle temptation of Satan. Why is this important? First, it qualified Jesus to be the pure sacrificial lamb who died in our place. In Hebrews 2:17, 18, we read: "Therefore he had to be made like his brethren in every respect, so that he might become a merciful and faithful high priest in the service of God, to make expiation for the sins of the people. For because he himself has suffered and been tempted, he is able to help those who are tempted." We know that we cannot withstand temptation. We fall together with Adam. But Jesus has withstood all temptation, and thus He is able to "stand in" for us.

Secondly, the way in which Jesus withstood temptation provided an example for us. He taught His disciples to pray, "And lead us not into temptation, But deliver us from evil" (Mt. 6:13). In the letter to the Philippians, we read, "Have this mind among yourselves, which is yours in Christ Jesus, who . . . did not count equality with God a thing to be grasped. . ." (Phil. 2:5, 6). The fact that Jesus did not seek to "become like God" is seen as a lesson for us. We are to be guided by His example. Thus the temptation of Jesus is important both for the remission of our sins and for our Christian walk. It is essential to keep our eyes on both aspects of this meaning for us.

It is significant that early in His ministry Jesus taught His disciples how to live. The Sermon on the Mount, recorded in the early pages of the Gospel of Matthew, is one example of His teachings. The Christian church has sometimes held that the guidelines given in the Sermon on the Mount do not apply to this life, but are meant for heaven. But this view misses the point of Jesus' ministry. He did not come only to die on the cross for our sins in order that we might consider ourselves justified even though we continue to sin. He also came in order to teach those who believe in Him to overcome sin through a new way of life. Nowhere did Jesus say or imply that the Sermon on the Mount was only for some future time. He took its precepts seriously for His own life, and at the same time "he said to all, 'If any man would come after me, let him deny himself and take up his cross daily and follow me'" (Lk. 9:23).

The Cross of Christ

The death of Jesus on the cross has been highlighted by Christians as the dramatic sign that He extends forgiveness to repentant sinners. The words of Romans 3:23-25 emphasize this point: "Since all have sinned and fall short of the glory of God, they are justified by his grace as a gift, through the redemption which is in Christ Jesus, whom God put forward as an expiation by his blood, to be received by faith." In Old Testament times sacrifices were prepared at certain times of the year. These were offered to God as an atonement for the sins of the people. Similarly the New Testament says that the death of Christ is an atoning sacrifice. However, Jesus is not just another sacrifice; He is the last and final all-sufficient sacrifice. That is, the sacrifice of God's Son is the sign that God's grace and mercy is available at all times and to everyone.

The emphasis upon the death of Christ as a sacrifice for our sins is, however, only one side of the coin. The cross has another meaning for our faith as well. It affords Christians an example of how we are to walk "in His steps." Not that we can thereby atone for our sins; Christ was a ransom for us once-for-all. Nonetheless, taking up our cross and following Christ faithfully cannot be separated from the gracious benefits bestowed upon us through His sacrificial death.

At times an attempt has been made to separate the double-sided teaching of the cross. Martin Luther has been credited with restoring the emphasis upon "justification by faith alone." By this he meant that there is nothing man can do to earn salvation. In making his point, however, he tended to lose sight of the other side of the coin. He played down the importance of our obedient response to Christ's work. This is seen in that Luther was critical of the Book of James where we read that "faith apart from works is dead" (2:26). Dietrich Bonhoeffer, writing in *The Cost of Discipleship* in the 1930s, spoke against a view of the cross which omits the emphasis upon being cross-bearing disciples. Grace without responsible discipleship is "cheap grace." In the same vein, Hans Denck, one of the Anabaptists of the sixteenth century, said, "No one knows Christ truly except he follow Him in life."

It has not been, and never will be, a simple matter to keep this double-sided understanding in balance. On the one hand, there will be the tendency to make too much of our works. This would take us in the direction of self-righteousness, salvation by works, a "holier-than-thou" attitude, and—eventually—humanism. On the other hand, there will be the tendency to speak of salvation only in terms of Christ's work for us, and not at all of our involvement in the process. This would take us in the direction of a faith separated from faithfulness. In the extreme, this direction is expressed in terms of sinning so "that grace may abound" (Rom. 6:1). This is also a foolish extreme. The truth of salvation is to be found in a balanced emphasis upon forgiveness and discipleship. The heart of the matter is expressed clearly in 2 Corinthians 5:18—"All this is from God, who through Christ reconciled us to himself and gave us the ministry of reconciliation. . . ."

Universal Salvation

In the above discussion we have focused on the meaning of salvation for personal human life. Our discussion of the topic must include the larger umbrella under which our own experience of salvation is included. In the Bible the term *salvation* is used in a grandiose way to refer to what God is doing with His entire universe (notice especially Isaiah 40-66, Ephesians 1-3, Revelation 21). In creating the universe, God had a purpose in mind. This plan has been challenged in various ways by mankind. But God is still determined to carry through with His original purpose. He will bring His intended work of salvation to completion. Even now His heavenly vision for the world is being carried forward in space and time. People have the option of whether or not they wish to participate in God's work. It appears that some will and some will not. But this does not hinder God in any final way. His work of salvation, which consequently includes the word of judgment, will endure.

TOPICS FOR DISCUSSION
1. The importance of the following for our salvation: Jesus' life, His cross, His resurrection.
2. Salvation as both a cosmic and a personal event.
3. Salvation through faith or through works?
4. The relationship between "evangelism" and "social concern."
5. Where does your life touch the theme of salvation?

SELECTED SCRIPTURE PASSAGES
Philippians 2:1-13
Ephesians 1 to 3
Romans 8

AIDS TO REFLECTION
"The name Jesus means Saviour . . . He not only saves us from something but also saves us for something. When driving through a strange country, a good guide can save us much time, worry and perhaps disappointment—indeed he can keep us from getting lost—simply by pointing out the right way. Jesus does this for us. Life is a strange territory and there are many roads, some lead downward to destruction and others lead upward to usefulness and happiness. Jesus is the good guide. He knows the way. But more than that—He is the way." Edmund G. Kaufman, *Basic Christian Convictions* (North Newton, Kans.: Bethel College, 1972), p. 162.

"Some may answer: Our belief is that Christ is the Son of God, that His Word is truth, and that He purchased us with His blood and truth. We were regenerated in baptism and we received the Holy Ghost; therefore we are the true church and congregation of Christ.
    We reply: If your faith is as you say, why do you not do the things which He has commanded you in His Word? His commandment is, Repent and keep the commandments. And it is evident that you grow worse daily; that unrighteousness is your father, wickedness your mother, and that the express commandments of the Lord are folly and foolishness to you. Since you do not do as He commands and desires, but as you please, it is sufficiently proved that you do not believe that Jesus Christ is the Son of God, although you say so. Nor do you believe that His Word is truth, for faith and its fruits are inseparable. This you will all have to confess by the grace of God." Menno Simons, "The New Birth," in *The Complete Writings of Menno Simons*, edited by J. C. Wenger (Scottdale, Pa.: Herald Press, 1956), p. 96.

"The reorientation of all human life in a direction which is not immediately perceptible to the natural intelligence of man, is a characteristic work of Christ as the Second Adam. It is the reparation of the harm done to the human race by Adam's fall. The Second Adam comes down to find man in the depths of confusion, in the moral chaos and disintegration into which he has been plunged by the sins of the first Adam and of all our other ancestors. Christ finds Adam, the "human race" like the Lost Sheep and carries him back by the way he came in his wandering from the truth. The substance of the mission of Christ is to unite men to Himself in the work by which God recommences, in the opposite direction the work undone by the first man." Thomas Merton, *The New Man* (New York: Mentor-Omega Books, 1963), p. 89.

FOR FURTHER READING

John R. Stott, *Basic Christianity.*

Robert H. Culpepper, *Interpreting the Atonement.* Grand Rapids: Eerdmans, 1966.

Vincent Taylor, *Forgiveness and Reconciliation.* London: Macmillan & Co., 1948.

9/HOLY SPIRIT

"But when the Counselor comes, whom I shall send to you from the Father, . . . he will bear witness to me." John 15:26

We believe in the Holy Spirit. What is meant by this? In simplest terms, *spirit* means "vigor" or "life." This is the root meaning of the word in the Old Testament. To have spirit was to have the breath of life. The wind was also referred to as spirit in the Old Testament. However the word *spirit* was most often used in a special sense to refer to God-given life. As such, spirit is not man-made, but is the gift of God.

There are varieties of spirits that influence people. Man is sometimes influenced by harmful spirits; at other times he yields to God's good Spirit. The psalmist prays: "Create in me a clean heart, O God, and put a new and right spirit within me. Cast me not away from thy presence, and take not thy holy Spirit from me" (Ps. 51:10, 11). The Holy Spirit is the Spirit of God which enables believers to have fellowship with the Lord and to mature in Christian life.

The prophets of the Old Testament hoped and prayed for a day when God would reveal himself clearly through His Spirit. It was discouraging for them to see the people being swayed by false prophets who were motivated by evil spirits. They were greatly encouraged when the divine promise came to them that God would make His will known through a Messiah who would be filled with the Spirit of the Lord:

> There shall come forth a shoot from the stump of Jesse,
> and a branch shall grow out of his roots.
> And the Spirit of the Lord shall rest upon him,
> the spirit of wisdom and understanding,
> the spirit of counsel and might,
> the spirit of knowledge and the fear of the Lord (Is. 11:1, 2).

In this Old Testament promise a person is envisioned who will embody the mysterious spirit of God in His life and teachings.

Jesus was the bearer of the promised Spirit of the Lord. In Him the Spirit of God was fully present. At the beginning of His ministry when He was baptized, John saw "the heavens opened and the Spirit descending upon him like a dove" (Mk. 1:10). Following His baptism, Jesus returned from the Jordan "full of the Holy Spirit" (Lk. 4:1). After His temptations He "returned in the power of the Spirit into Galilee" (Lk. 4:14). At Nazareth He read to the people from Isaiah 61:1, 2: "The Spirit of the Lord is upon me. . ." (Lk. 4:18). It is striking to note how the Spirit is concentrated in the person of Jesus, giving Him heavenly wisdom and power. He fulfills the expectation of the prophet Isaiah.

Thus if we want to know what the Holy Spirit is like, it is necessary to look to Jesus. The Holy Spirit is the Spirit of Jesus Christ. This is a great help to us, because it is sometimes very difficult to determine the true Spirit of God from false spirits in our day. How do you decide between the claims of two people if both insist they speak in accord with the Spirit of God, and yet the one claim is contrary to the other? The rule of thumb is that the authentic voice of the Holy Spirit will always be in agreement with the Spirit of Jesus as we know this from what He said and did in His earthly ministry (Jn. 16:14). We do not need to think of the Holy Spirit as sheer incomprehensible power. The Spirit is clothed with the personality and the character of Jesus. We can think of Jesus as the window through whom the Spirit is seen by us and as the channel through whom the Spirit comes to us.

The Promise of the Spirit

When Jesus walked upon the earth, He was readily available to the people who gathered around Him. He could teach them, answer their questions, and demonstrate His message through His deeds. This was of great advantage to His followers because they could hear Him directly on this or that issue of the day, and they could see for themselves just how to put the good news into practice.

However, it became obvious as His life progressed that He could not remain on earth forever. The Father had a greater plan in mind for Him. At the same time, there was growing hatred of Him to the extent that some were plotting His death. Jesus would soon leave His little flock.

In one way this was unfortunate; it would have been good for the disciples to have their Master with them for many years to come. However, the fact that Jesus would soon leave the scene, at least in His present earthly form, had its positive side as well. In discussing the matter of leaving the disciples, Jesus said: ". . . It is to your advantage that I go away, for if I do not go away, the Counselor [Holy Spirit] will not come to you; but if I go, I will send him to you" (Jn. 16:7). Upon Jesus' return to the Father, the Holy Spirit would be sent to guide and teach Christians. This would be an advantage to

His followers, since the Spirit is not limited to one place as the earthly Jesus was.

If we start with the basic principle that the Father has chosen to work patiently over a long period of time with His children, then even the time that Jesus spent on earth was not long enough to say and do all that needed to be accomplished. In His last days on earth Jesus said: "I have yet many things to say to you, but you cannot bear them now. When the Spirit of truth comes, he will guide you into all the truth. . . . He will glorify me, for he will take what is mine and declare it to you" (Jn. 16:12-14). That is, Jesus has continued and expanded His work throughout history and in the present through His Spirit, the Holy Spirit.

Through the Holy Spirit things have been taught to Christians which Jesus did not teach while on earth. This is true in a very practical sense in the history of the Christian church. The good news about Jesus has been carried to many corners of the earth and has inspired words and actions which the very first disciples would never have imagined to be possible. As time and culture change and progress throughout history, new situations call for new ways of expressing the Christian message. It is the work of the Holy Spirit both to inspire the growth of the Christian message from age to age, and to ensure that the original intent of the message as Jesus expressed it is preserved.

The Baptism of the Spirit

In Christian circles there is discussion at times as to who possesses the Holy Spirit and who does not. This is a very important issue, since it influences our attitude toward one another, and our expectations of one another. Two expressions are often used in this context: "baptized with the Spirit" and "filled with the Spirit." Do these describe special experiences of certain people, or are they common to all Christians?

In the Old Testament there is the promise of a day when the Lord will pour out his spirit on all people (Joel 2:28, 29). Here the idea is that the Lord will shower His grace and goodness on the entire earth, and that the Spirit of God with its accompanying goodness and justice will be evidenced not in a few chosen Israelites, but in all people, Jews and Gentiles.

When John the Baptist arrived on the scene, the people asked whether he was the one who would bring in this new age. He answered: "After me comes one who is mightier than I. . . . I have baptized you with water; but he will baptize you with the Holy Spirit" (Mk. 1:7, 8). Thereupon Jesus was baptized with water by John. At the same time the Spirit descended upon Him (Mk. 1:10). What does this mean? It meant that Jesus was the person through whom the outpouring of the Spirit, as prophesied by Joel, was now about to take place. Quite specifically, this meant that the blessing of God was now available to "all flesh." Everyone, regardless of race or color, whether Jew or Gentile, could claim a right to the grace of God on an equal basis. Jesus emphasized this work of the Spirit in His ministry. He invited not only Jews, but Gentiles as well, to follow Him. He forgave the sins of all who repented. He asked every person—king and pauper, rich and poor, male and female—to serve one another. The baptism of the Holy Spirit is available to all persons through Jesus Christ. This point is emphasized on the Day of Pentecost when the word of God was heard by people representing a great variety of nations and languages (Acts 2:8-12).

Notice how closely water baptism and spirit baptism are associated in Jesus' experience. Can we say the same for today? In Ezekiel 36:25, 27, the following promise is given: "I will sprinkle clean water upon you, and you shall be clean. . . . And I will put my spirit within you, and cause you to walk in my statutes and be careful to observe my ordinances." Sprinkling (baptism) with water and the reception of a new spirit are in continuity here. The same can be said for the baptism of Jesus. When Jesus stepped out of the Jordan after being baptized with water by John, the Spirit descended upon Him (Mk. 1:10). Similarly, on the day of Pentecost the Apostle Peter proclaimed this double-sided baptism: "Repent, and be baptized every one of you in the name of Jesus Christ for the forgiveness of your sins; and you shall receive the gift of the Holy Spirit" (Acts 2:38).

The foregoing discussion says three things to us about baptism by the Holy Spirit. First, Holy Spirit baptism is available to everyone. It is not a special gift for a chosen few. Rather, it is a universal Christian experience. Second, baptism of the Holy Spirit is experienced when the person becomes a Christian and is baptized by water. That is, it is a normal part of the experience of confessing Christ. The gift of the Holy Spirit is in principle an initial Christian experience. Water baptism is a public act of initiation into Christ. As such it signifies both cleansing from sin and the reception of the Holy Spirit. There may be individual cases where the Spirit is not welcomed into one's life when one is baptized, but this should be the exception rather than the expectation. Third, baptism of the Spirit is linked particularly with sanctification—that is, with a life of obedience to God. This last point brings us to a consideration of the expression "the fullness of the Holy Spirit."

Filled with the Spirit

The expression "filled with the Spirit" refers to the ongoing dimension of the Christian life. It is the will of God that Christians experience the presence of the Holy Spirit continually. Love for God and for our neighbor are the signs of the Spirit's presence. We know from experience that Christian life has its ups and downs, and hence we cannot claim to be filled with the Spirit continually. To some extent our attitude of heart and our acts determine whether or not the Spirit is allowed to dwell in us. From God's standpoint the Spirit is available, but from our own standpoint there is not always room for the Spirit. It should be the hope and prayer of Christians that the Spirit of God may be continuously and increasingly appropriated.

In addition to the continuous presence of the Spirit, the Spirit also works at special times and in special ways. Some persons are "filled with the Holy Spirit" in order to do a special task, such as preaching, prophesying, healing. (See 1 Corinthians 12:4-10.) The striking emphasis in the New Testament, however, is on the servant character of these special gifts. The individual endowments of the Spirit are given, not for individuals to put themselves above others, but in order to serve one another. To "be filled with the Spirit" (Eph. 5:18) is to "be subject to one another out of reverence for Christ" (5:21). This becomes abundantly clear in the Apostle Paul's discussion of the gifts of Spirit in the Corinthian church (see 1 Corinthians 12 and 13) where the apostle admonishes those who claim to have special gifts to place the gift of love above all others.

The question of who has a special measure of the Spirit and who does not is answered by the New Testament on the basis of the fruits of the Christian life. Time and results will tell the story. Where there is "love, joy, peace, patience, kindness, goodness, faithfulness, gentleness, self-control" (Gal. 5:22, 23a), the Spirit is present. Thus the question of who is "filled with the Spirit" cannot be settled by argument but by the fruits of Christian living.

TOPICS FOR DISCUSSION
1. The biblical teaching concerning the Spirit of God.
2. Is the Holy Spirit the Spirit of Jesus?
3. Pentecost as an ongoing event.
4. Where do you experience the Holy Spirit: in community; in the inward life; in the world?

SELECTED SCRIPTURE PASSAGES
Galatians 5
Acts 2:1-42
John 16:1-15

AIDS TO REFLECTION
"The Spirit of God which appeared fitfully, in a variety of forms, and prophetically in the Old Testament days shone steadily, personally, and fully in the Man of Nazareth. No longer is the Holy Spirit encountered as naked power; he is clothed with the personality and character of Jesus. If you like, Jesus is the funnel through whom the Spirit becomes available to men. Jesus transposes the Spirit into a fully personal key. Jesus is the prism through whom the diffused and fitful light of the Spirit is concentrated. Jesus is *the* prophet (Luke 7:16, Acts 3:22, 7:37) the long-awaited prophet of the endtime, through whom the prophetic Spirit, so active in the Old Testament, gave full and final revelation. We have seen that Jesus gave this Spirit to his disciples in virtue of, and subsequent to his death and resurrection. What follows is that the Spirit is for ever afterwards marked with the character of Jesus. Indeed, he can be called 'the Spirit of Jesus' (Acts 16:7)." Michael Green, *I Believe in the Holy Spirit* (Grand Rapids: Wm. B. Eerdmans, 1975), p. 42.

"The Christian life is life in the Spirit. All Christians are happily agreed about this. It would be impossible to be a Christian, let alone to live and grow as a Chrsitian, without the ministry of the gracious Spirit of God. All we have and are as Christians we owe to him. So every Christian believer has an experience of the Holy Spirit from the very first moments of his Christian life. For the Christian life begins with a new birth, and the new birth is a birth 'of the Spirit' (Jn. 3:3-8). He is 'the Spirit of life', and it is he who imparts life to our dead souls. More than this, he comes himself to dwell within us, and the indwelling of the Spirit is the common possession of all God's children." John R. W. Stott, *Baptism and Fulness* (Leicester, England: Inter-Varsity Press, 1964), p. 19.

"The drama of incarnation does not conclude with a final act that neatly wraps up the loose ends of the story and draws the curtain. Rather it ends with an open future for those involved. Pentecost is a commencement in the same sense that we use the word to describe a graduation. It is simultaneously climax and beginning. . . . Christ is not dead or absent in some far-off spiritual realm. The kingdom he announced is not set aside to some future millennium but enters a new era of fulfillment. His ministry is not concluded but universalized through his new body. Surely this is part of the good news!" C. Norman Kraus, *The Community of the Spirit* (Grand Rapids: Eerdmans, 1974), p. 12.

FOR FURTHER READING

Michael Green, *I Believe in the Holy Spirit.* Grand Rapids: Eerdmans, 1975.
Myron Augsburger, *Quench Not the Spirit.* Scottdale, Pa.: Herald Press, 1961.
H. Wheeler Robinson, *The Christian Experience of the Holy Spirit.* London: Collins, 1962.
John R. Stott, *Baptism and Fulness.* Downers Grove, Ill.: Inter-Varsity Press, 1976.

10/BECOMING CHRISTIAN

"If any man would come after me, let him deny himself and take up his cross daily and follow me. For whoever would save his life will lose it; and whoever loses his life for my sake, he will save it." *Luke 9:23, 24*

At the center of our Christian faith stands the crucial question: What must I do to be saved? In one sense the answer to this question is quite straightforward: "Believe on the Lord Jesus Christ, and thou shalt be saved" (Acts 16:31, KJV). However, while this is the standard and fundamental answer to the question, there have been a variety of interpretations and additional requirements added by various groups of Christians. For this reason we need to provide an extended explanation of what it means to be saved.

Some people attribute their decision for Christ totally to a "moment of decision"; others testify to a gradual process of growth under the influence of Christian parents. Both of these have validity. Most persons have become Christians through a combination of decision making and gradual growth. The Scriptures provide us with illustrations of both. Paul, the apostle, had a radical conversion experience. Timothy, his young co-worker, apparently was drawn to Christ through the nurture which he enjoyed in the home. No doubt Paul also thought of himself as continuing to become "more Christian" as he matured in Christ. On the other hand, it is quite likely that Timothy would be able to point to occasions in his life when he became particularly conscious of the necessity of deciding for his Lord. It is not enough to only say yes to the faith of our parents. We need to decide whether or not what they believe will become our personal faith as well.

It is instructive to note that the Greek verb for "to be saved" in the New Testament often has the idea of continuity. That is, it is translated variously as "was being saved" (continuous action in the past), "am being saved" (continuous action in the present), and "will be saved" (continuous action in the future). Here the emphasis is on a process beginning in the past, continuing in the present, and stretching into the future. Thus a Christian should recognize that he is engaged in a process of ongoing growth. For many there has been an identifiable starting point when through repentance and faith the decision was made to be "in Christ." From that point on, however, one can speak of continually becoming a Christian. This is a process which is not completed until we become one with Christ in the future.

A word of caution should be given to persons who attribute their Christian status to a radical once-for-all decision. We cannot underestimate the subtle influences that have prepared us for the momentous decision for Christ. For some this influence has come through Christian parents and through a process of Sunday school instruction. For others there have been important words of encouragement in early childhood and later. As Christians we need to cultivate an appreciation for the many persons through whom the Spirit of God works patiently and slowly. Conversion includes a process of becoming.

Believe

In simplest terms a Christian is a person who believes that Jesus of Nazareth is the Christ sent by the Father as Savior and Lord. On the day of Pentecost, some days after Jesus' death and resurrection, the disciple Peter preached a sermon in which he made the radical claim that Jesus, who had recently been put to death on the cross, had been raised from the dead, and that "God has made him both Lord and Christ" (Acts 2:36). Peter's audience believed this and were very dismayed at the thought, since they and their fellow citizens of Jerusalem had been involved in such a terrible act. While the hearers may not have participated directly in the crucifixion, they accepted responsibility for this bad deed by virture of being fellow citizens with all in Jerusalem. Thus they "were cut to the heart, and said to Peter and the rest of the apostles, 'Brethren, what shall we do?'" (Acts 2:37). Peter's answer was quick in coming: "Repent, and be baptized. . ." (2:38). God will forgive you for this awful deed if you are truly sorry, and if you change your mind regarding Jesus of Nazareth. He was not a blasphemer and naughty troublemaker as many had claimed. Rather, He was the Messiah sent by God. This decision regarding Jesus became the turning point for the people.

One can say on the basis of the report in Acts 2 that to be counted as a Christian is to believe that Jesus of Nazareth is the Christ, the Son of God, our Lord and Savior, and to repent for the awful death of Jesus. We were there when Jesus was crucified by virtue of belonging to the human race, part of which was directly active in putting Jesus to death. Happily, God turned the event into a blessing for us, and that is cause for abundant thanksgiving.

Repent

Becoming a Christian means coming to terms with that aspect of ourselves which is rooted in sinfulness, asking God to forgive us and to replace our sinful nature with a Christlike nature. The letter to the Romans is especially emphatic on the point that fundamentally every human being is a sinner. There is no one that can claim to be "godly" in all aspects of personal being. Some might want to argue that man cannot be called a sinner until he is proven to be one through his acts. However, this is too individualistic a view of human nature. I am what I am only partly by virtue of what I do. In part, I am also of one piece with all humanity. As a member of the human race, I share in its activity. Already at birth I "inherit" what has happened before I was born. This becomes evident in a concrete way when, as a growing child, I readily adopt many of the ways of mankind. And if it is not evident in childhood, then certainly by the time of youth and adulthood it becomes apparent that the history and environment created by humanity is of one piece with many aspects of my nature. Some of this influence is for good; some is for ill. In any case, I must confess that I am part, not only of the good, but certainly also of the evil nature of mankind.

It is this reality that I must face and come to grips with. The Christian admits that "all have sinned and fall short of the glory of God" (Rom. 3:23). To admit this in the name of Jesus Christ is to be "united with him in a death like his" (Rom. 6:5), to allow our old self to be "crucified with him so that the sinful body might be destroyed, and we might no longer be enslaved to sin" (6:6). In this way our sins are removed by identification with the death of Jesus on the cross.

Having admitted this, the Christian is committed to promoting the righteousness of God in the face of worldly evil. The point is expressed well in Romans 6:22—"But now that you have been set free from sin and have become slaves of God, the return you get is sanctification and its end, eternal life." To live in this new way is spoken of in Romans as being "united with [Christ] in a resurrection like his" (6:5). As persons who have died with Christ, "you also must consider yourselves dead to sin and alive to God in Christ Jesus" (6:11). In short, to become a Christian a person needs to accept the sacrificial death and the renewing resurrection of Jesus Christ as a meaningful symbol for his or her own life.

Very often a presentation on what it means to be saved ends at this point with the assumption that little more needs to be said. It is assumed that the question of salvation is the question of what to do about our sinful natures. Certainly this is an important part of the matter, but it is not the whole of it. To stop at this point would be to stop short of the biblical view of becoming a Christian. Thus we move to a further point.

Follow

Following in the steps of Jesus belongs to the process of becoming a Christian. This point gains firm support from Jesus himself. On one occasion a man asked Him, "Good Teacher, what must I do to inherit eternal life?" After some discussion, Jesus answered his question: "Go, sell what you have, and give to the poor, and you will have treasure in heaven; and come, follow me" (Mk. 10:17, 21). The disciples were troubled by Jesus' hard demand; thus, they asked, "Then who can be saved?" (10:26). Jesus' answer is significant: "With men it is impossible, but not with God; for all things are possible with God" (10:27). This means that discipleship, or following Jesus, is not to be thought of as a joyless self-achievement, but as a joyful participation in the work and will of God, who will provide the strength for the disciple's commitment. There is the constant danger that an emphasis upon following Jesus can become "salvation by works." Jesus is not calling for man to earn his righteousness. On the other hand He obviously understands "works" as a part of the redeeming intention of God. In 1 John 4:7 we read that "he who loves is born of God." It is important to emphasize that as we follow Christ, it is not that we gain merit in the eyes of God. Rather our discipleship constitutes a responsive thank-you to God, expressed as a participation in His larger work in the universe.

One of our Mennonite leaders, Myron Augsburger, wrote a book several years ago which he entitled *Invitation to Discipleship*. The subtitle of the book is *The Message of Evangelism*. This illustrates very well the point that is being made by Jesus. The message of evangelism includes the invitation to discipleship. Furthermore, the term *discipleship* must not be understood too narrowly. There is a tendency among some Christians to think of discipleship only as the task of inviting others to be saved. This is certainly a part of the task. But it includes a much broader range of activities as well. Any activity which promotes the work of the kingdom of God, such as showing mercy, promoting justice, healing, and preaching peace, is included.

Fellowship

Becoming a Christian involves association with the Christian congregation, the church. As Mennonites we have held that one cannot be a Christian in isolation. Rather one seeks the fellowship of those who belong to "the body of Christ." God has chosen to express His work of salvation primarily in and through the church. Thus it is in this context that we are able to taste and see the goodness of the Lord and to experience "Christian becoming" in greater measure. That is why the rite of baptism is related closely with church membership. It is our conviction that the baptismal testimony of the experience of salvation must be inseparably linked to the commitment to a local congregation and to the universal body of Christ on earth.

What Must I Do?

Perhaps it would be helpful, in conclusion, to summarize by stating a sequence of five steps to follow in becoming a Christian:

1. Confess that in your deepest being you are one with Adam's race. Thus you are responsible with Adam in his Fall, and you are responsible together with those who denied Jesus as the Christ. Admit your guilt, ask the Father to forgive you, and accept His guarantee of forgiveness. Enjoy the fact that in God through Christ you are accepted just as you are.

2. Resolve to follow Christ in life, not as a way of gaining favor with God, but as a joyous response to His grace and will. Expect that you will not find the Christian way to be "a bed of roses." There will be high points and low points. Be assured that Christ is your Comforter and Guide.

3. Join the fellowship of believers through baptism. Consider yourself a Christian fellow-worker with a contribution to make as well as something to gain from fellow Christians. Be ready to receive and to give counsel. Do not become discouraged if the church is not perfect. You would feel out of place if it were.

4. Witness to your faith in Christ as you are able and as God gives opportunity. Do so through word and through deed. Rely on the strength and guidance of the Holy Spirit as you prepare to share

your faith.

5. Pray for the final dawn of the kingdom of God at the end of this age. Live in the hope that Christ will reveal His Lordship over earth and heaven in His own good time.

TOPICS FOR DISCUSSION
1. The biblical idea of what it means to be saved.
2. New Testament illustrations of decision making: the disciples, Paul, the residents of Thessalonica (Acts 17:1ff.).
3. The problem of a one-sided interpretation which focuses only on forgiveness or only on good works.
4. The place of Jesus' invitation to "follow Me" in becoming a Christian.
5. Are we drawn to Christ through fear or through love?

SELECTED SCRIPTURE PASSAGES
John 3:1-21
Acts 9:1-31
Romans 5 and 6
Matthew 19:16-30

AIDS TO REFLECTION
"Five years ago faith came to me; I believed in the doctrine of Jesus, and my whole life underwent a sudden transformation. What I had once wished for I wished for no longer, and I began to desire what I had never desired before. What had once appeared to me as right now became wrong, and the wrong of the past I beheld as right. . . . My life and my desires were completely changed; good and evil inter-changed meanings." Leo Tolstoi, *My Religion.*

"The salvation of which Jesus was 'pioneer and perfecter' is described in a rich variety of metaphors drawn from everyday life in the ancient world. There are the ritual metaphors of washing, sacrifice, and consecration. There are figures associated with freedom—redemption from bondage to an alien law and ransom from slavery to sin and Satan. There are the references to salvation as new life—new birth, resurrection, new creation, and regeneration. Salvation is changing one's whole way of thinking and turning in a new direction—repentance and conversion. It is a renewal and reorientation of life. It means release from the guilt of sin and reconciliation with God and man—forgiveness, justification, and 'peace with God through our Lord, Jesus Christ.' None of these may be used exclusively to present a theology of salvation. Rather they are like the facets of a superb and finely polished diamond which reflect back the brilliance of God's revelation in Christ." C. Norman Kraus, *The Community of the Spirit* (Grand Rapids: Eerdmans, 1974), p. 50.

"Not all conversions come as a sudden, brilliant flash of soul illumination that we call a crisis conversion. There are many others that are accomplished only after a long and difficult conflict with the inner motives of the person. With others, conversion comes as the climactic moment of a long period of gradual conviction of their need and revelation of the plan of salvation. This prolonged process results in conscious acceptance of Christ as personal Savior and in the yielding of life to Him." Billy Graham, *Peace with God* (Garden City, N.Y.: Doubleday & Company, Inc., 1953), p. 106.

FOR FURTHER READING

John H. Westerhoff, *Will Our Children Have Faith?* New York: The Seabury Press, 1976.

William Barclay, *Turning to God.* London: Epworth, 1963.

Samuel Shoemaker, *How to Become a Christian.* New York: Harper, 1953.

11/BAPTISM AND COMMUNION

We were buried therefore with him by baptism into death, so that as Christ was raised from the dead by the glory of the Father, we too might walk in newness of life. Romans 6:4

Baptism and communion (the Lord's Supper) are ordinances. That is, they are practices prescribed in the New Testament. In the Great Commission we read, "Make disciples of all nations, baptizing them. . ." (Mt. 28:19); with reference to the last supper which Jesus held with His disciples, we read, "Do this in remembrance of me" (1 Cor. 11:24). Some Mennonite groups practice only these two ordinances. Others add foot washing and the love feast.

The underlying reason for the practice of baptism and communion is deeper than mere ritualistic prescription. Both practices symbolize the unity of the believers with the Lord at the most crucial point of His life—suffering and death. In speaking of His coming death, Jesus said, "I have a baptism to be baptized with" (Lk. 12:50). The communion meal was held on the eve of His suffering and death. When His disciples were following Him to Jerusalem, He confronted them with the hard question, "Are you able to *drink the cup* that I drink, or to *be baptized* with the baptism with which I am baptized?" (Mk. 10:38.) Notice the symbolic use of baptism and communion in this statement.

The ordinances of baptism and communion are also symbolic of the unity of believers with one another. First Corinthians 12:13 affirms this interpretation: "For by one Spirit we were all *baptized* into one body—Jews or Greeks, slaves or free—and all were made to *drink* of one Spirit." Thus the unity of the church with Christ and with one another is uppermost in our minds and hearts when we participate in baptism and communion.

How Baptism Began

From the beginning of the history of religion man has made use of earthly materials to express religious devotion. When Abraham made a covenant with the Lord, he sacrificed animals. When the people of Israel wanted to say thank-you to God for leading them to the Promised Land, they gathered stones and built an altar. When man has wished to symbolize his religious sentiments, appropriate materials were usually at hand. These assisted in expressing devotion to God and in lending concreteness and seriousness to commitments.

It is quite understandable that water has become a widespread and important religious symbol. Water plays an important role in the day-to-day life of all peoples. One of its main uses is for cleaning. In this connection it is significant that in biblical times water was used in rituals as a symbol of purification. For example, when a leper was healed of disease, he underwent a ritual washing to symbolize that he was clean (Lev. 14:9). The practice of ritual cleansing from sin is indicated in Psalm 51:2—"Wash me thoroughly from my iniquity, and cleanse me from my sin!" Similarly, the prophets linked washing with the forgiveness of sin. The prophet Ezekiel conveys the following promise from the Lord: "I will sprinkle clean water upon you, and you shall be clean from all your uncleannesses, and from all your idols I will cleanse you" (Ezek. 36:25). In the Qumran community in which the recently discovered Dead Sea Scrolls originate, there were many cistern-like baths which were used daily for purification ceremonies.

This emphasis upon purification through water is a preparation for what we find in the New Testament. When we turn to the opening verses of the Gospel of Mark, we read of John the baptizer preaching a message of repentance and baptizing people as a symbolic act signifying the forgiveness of their sins. John's message was aimed at the religious Jews of his day. He asked them to accept baptism as a preparation for a greater revelation of God: "I baptize you with water for repentance, but he who is coming after me is mightier than I . . . ; he will baptize you with the Holy Spirit and with fire" (Mt. 3:11). John's baptism was not only a baptism for forgiveness of sins. It was also an opening of the door to a life of commitment to the works of the kingdom. He called his followers to "bear fruits that befit repentance" (Lk. 3:8). The newly baptized converts were reminded not to rest on the fact that they were Jews by birth (Abraham's children—Lk. 3:8). Rather they were to form a new community of the committed, based not on their birthright but on a responsible commitment to the Lord. Thus baptism is not only a symbol of cleansing from sin; it is also a symbol of commitment to new life.

The Baptism of Jesus

It is somewhat of a surprise that Jesus presented himself for baptism by John as well. He didn't need to repent; and surely His commitment to the will of God could be taken for granted. It is understandable that John, pointing to Jesus as the Lamb of God, hesitated to baptize Him. John says, "I need to be baptized by you, and do you come to me?" (Mt. 3:14.) Yet Jesus insisted on being baptized. Three reasons can be suggested for this. First, Jesus wanted to identify with His people—with those who repented and joined the community of the righteous. Second, Jesus wanted to identify himself as the promised Messiah of the Old Testament. The word *messiah* literally means "the anointed one." Jesus' baptism can be viewed as an anointing for His messianic role. Third, Jesus' baptism can be seen as an act of consecration to the will of God. It stands at the beginning of His ministry as an "ordination service."

Thus Jesus' baptism fits into the orderly scheme of the work of God in salvation history. In one way Jesus' baptism is special, since it is the Son of God who is being baptized here. In another sense, however, His baptism is united with our baptism. Our baptism, like His, is an act of consecration to a future task. Also, our baptism, like His, symbolizes our entry into the community of faith.

Baptism in the Early Church

When we turn to the rest of the New Testament, several points can be made about Christian baptism. We note first that baptism was commanded by Jesus. Just before His ascension He spoke these words to His disciples: "All authority in heaven and on earth has been given to me. Go therefore and make disciples of all nations, baptizing them in the name of the Father and of the Son and of the Holy Spirit" (Mt. 28:18, 19). Notice how the activities of discipling and teaching are bound up with baptizing. The act of baptizing thus plays an important role in Christian growth.

Baptism is a double sign, pointing to a past act of repentance from sin and to a present and future commitment to Christ and the cause of His church. In Acts 2 we read that those who repented were baptized (2:38, 41), and thereupon they devoted themselves to the teachings of Jesus and to the fellowship of fellow believers (2:42). Thus baptism serves as both a seal or stamp of approval from God and an "ordination" to Christian service.

In the letters of Paul, the act of baptism is seen as a miniature drama which depicts important elements of the Christian life. In Romans 6:3-11 it is emphasized that our baptism signifies our unity with Christ in His death. In Galatians 3:27 it is said that to be baptized is to "put on Christ" in life.

It seems clear that baptism was entered into by maturing

individuals who were aware of the responsible step they were taking. They were conscious of their sin and had committed themselves initially to Jesus Christ. Some theologians argue that small children were baptized in the early church, since we read that the Philippian jailer was baptized "with all his family" (Acts 16:33). There is the slim possibility that this could have been the case. Yet the dominant emphasis in the New Testament is on baptism as a result of mature commitment on the part of the recipient. This is explainable to some extent because all believers in the New Testament were of the first generation. Yet it seems reasonable to assume that baptism was not thought of as an automatic rite to be given to children upon their parents' confession of faith. Rather, each person has the right and responsibility to decide for or against baptism.

The form of baptism is not an important issue in the New Testament. Marcus Barth, a New Testament theologian, says that there were probably many forms used in the early history of the church. Whether you sprinkle water on the head, or pour it on, or immerse the person is not the crucial question. Of crucial importance is the meaning that is given to the ritual by the one being baptized and by the church. Those who argue for immersion point to the words in Romans 6:4: "We were buried . . . by baptism into death." Those who argue for sprinkling or pouring link baptism with the Old Testament practice of anointing or of sprinkling the blood of the sacrificial lamb on the people. Throughout church history both means have been used. As church denominations we do well not to let the particular mode of baptism divide us. At the same time, it is best if those who are baptized in a particular church accept the form that is used in that church. Otherwise one would be making an issue of the form.

Anabaptist Baptism

One of the critical factors in the birth of the Mennonite church was the issue of baptism. It had been the practice for years in the Roman Catholic church to administer baptism to infants. The baptismal water was administered to wash away the sin which every person inherited from Adam. It was believed that an infant would likely not go to heaven if it died before baptism could be administered. The Lutheran and Zwinglian reformers did not seriously challenge this view. But a group of radical reformers did. Conrad Grebel and his companions questioned the practice of infant baptism. They argued that the New Testament gives no basis for baptizing infants. As far as infants and children are concerned, they said, Christ's atonement preserved them from judgment during the age of innocence. Anabaptist forefathers insisted, further, that a conscious inner transformation of the heart must precede baptism. They spoke of baptism as a covenant between man and God, and between fellow believers in the church. Thus it is properly administered only after children have grown into youth or adulthood, and only upon a personal confession of sin and commitment to Christ and His cause.

In 1527 a crucial meeting of radical reformers took place at Schleitheim in Switzerland. By this time there were many different opinions in the movement, and it was considered necessary to try to resolve these. Seven points of discussion were dealt with, and there was agreement on each point. It is significant that the first of the seven articles concerned baptism. The statement in the Schleitheim Confession reads as follows:

> Baptism shall be given to all those who have been taught repentance and the amendment of life and who believe truly that their sins are taken away through Christ, and to all those who desire to walk in the resurrection of Jesus Christ and be buried with Him in death, so that they might rise with Him; to all those who with such an understanding themselves desire and request it from us; hereby is excluded all infant baptism, the greatest and first abomination of the pope. For this you have the reasons and the testimony of the writings and the practice of the apostles. We wish simply yet resolutely and with assurance to hold to the same. [1]

But that does not complete the story. Already the earliest leaders and followers of this movement were being persecuted for their faith. They were nicknamed "Anabaptists" (which means "rebaptizers") because they rejected their first baptism as infants and baptized one another a second time. The practice was soon outlawed by the church and state of the day. Already in 1527 Michael Sattler, an ex-monk who had turned Anabaptist, was tried in Rottenburg and burned at the stake. The issue of baptism was a matter of life and death to our spiritual forefathers.

Baptism Today

The Mennonite church has held to the practice of adult baptism throughout the centuries since the sixteenth century. In the meantime many other denominations, such as the Baptist church, have also practiced believer's baptism. However, it is not a simple matter to maintain the emphasis upon the baptismal act that the Anabaptists gained for us through suffering and death. There is the constant temptation to ask for baptism because our parents desire it or because our friends are being baptized or because "it's the thing to do" at a certain age. While these motivating factors are not all wrong, they should not dominate our decision for baptism. The request for baptism must grow out of a personal confession of sin and a commitment to Jesus Christ and to the congregation.

The Communion Service

When we participate in the communion service, we notice at once the centrality of the bread and the wine. Some denominations have a somewhat mystical view of these elements. The Roman Catholic church believes that the bread and wine are mysteriously changed into the flesh and blood of Christ during the service. Thus in the very eating and drinking, the believers are united with Christ. Other groups, such as the Lutherans, say that in the act of eating the bread and drinking the wine, the believer becomes spiritually united with Christ. The Catholic view is known as *transubstantiation;* the Lutheran emphasis is called *consubstantiation.*

The Mennonite church takes a less mystical and more realistic view of the elements. The communion service is a meal of remembrance. As such, it points participants to the past, the present, and the future.

As a meal reminding us of the *past,* the communion service takes us back to the Jewish Passover festival. Here bread and wine were used to remind the people of the manna that God had supplied during the wanderings in the wilderness, and the blood of the paschal lamb that was slain on the night that the Israelites in Egypt were spared from the angel of death. When Jesus shared the passover meal with His disciples on the night that He was betrayed, He gave these symbols new meaning. Of the bread He said, "This is my body" (Mt. 26:26). With reference to the wine, He said, "This is my blood of the covenant" (26:28). When His followers partake of the elements, they are reminded that He gave His life for our deliverance. Thus the death of Christ broadens the experience of deliverance from bondage to include not only Israelites, but all nations.

The communion service also serves to focus our attention upon the *present*. There is the reality of present fellowship with Christ as we partake. In calling to memory the person and death of Jesus Christ, we "feed on Him in our hearts." But the meal also focuses our attention on the joy and responsibility of fellowship with one another. In 1 Corinthians 10:17 we read, "Because there is one bread, we who are many are one body, for we all partake of the one bread." Thus the eating of the bread symbolizes Christian unity. In the same passage the Apostle Paul warns against eating and drinking "in an unworthy manner" (11:27). It is of no effect—indeed, it is profane—to partake of communion when there is division and strife among fellow believers (11:18-22). Thus it is appropriate that participants search their hearts and examine their relationships with one another to ensure that they are in Christlike harmony with fellow Christians, lest they make a farce of this very important event in the life of God's people. The communion service provides an occasion for testing our care for one another in the present life of the congregation.

In the Anabaptist-Mennonite tradition special emphasis is placed on the Lord's Supper as a fellowship meal. The meal symbolizes fellowship with Christ and with one another. Our forefathers liked to recall an old parable that appeared first in an ancient Christian manuscript, the *Didaché:*

As the grain-kernels are altogether merged and each must give its content or strength (*Vermögen*) into the one flour and bread, likewise also the wine, where the grapes are crushed under the press, and each grape gives away all its juice and all its strength into one wine. Whichever kernel and whichever grape, however, is not crushed and retains its strength for itself alone, such an one is unworthy and is cast out. This is what Christ wanted to bring home to His companions and guests at the Last Supper as an example of how they should be together in such a fellowship" (Andreas Ehrenpreis, 1652).[2]

Thus the communion service draws to our attention the quality of our present relationships with one another and with Christ.

The communion service also reminds us of the *future* goal of the Christian life. The New Testament speaks of the Lord's Supper as a proclamation of a future event: "For as often as you eat this bread and drink the cup, you proclaim the Lord's death until he comes" (1 Cor. 11:26). Gathering together for the simple communion service keeps the hope of the return of Christ alive among believers. The service is, in that connection, a foretaste of the great heavenly banquet. Appropriately, the emphasis is not upon great amounts of food and drink, but upon fellowship with the Lord and with the people of God.

In Conclusion

It is unfortunate that baptism and the communion service have sometimes been the cause for divisions between churches and among church members. These are the very occasions that should foster love and unity, as becomes clear when we examine the symbolic meaning of these celebrations. It is the responsibility of each new generation of believers to sense the meaning and the potential power of the ordinances, and to allow baptism and communion to provide a framework for daily experience.

TOPICS FOR DISCUSSION
1. The importance of baptism in the New Testament.
2. Why Jesus was baptized, and how our baptism relates to the baptism of Jesus.
3. Anabaptist-Mennonite understanding and experience of baptism.
4. Baptism as a dying and rising with Christ.
5. The meaning of the Lord's Supper in the Christian church.
6. The individual and communal responsibilities implied by partaking of communion.

SELECTED SCRIPTURE PASSAGES
Romans 6:1-11
Mark 1:9-11
Mark 10:35-40
Colossians 2:12

AIDS TO REFLECTION

"The outstanding characteristic of Mennonite groups continues to be today, as it was in its beginning, a voluntary church made up of believers who have placed their faith and trust in Jesus Christ. Only those who are old enough to decide carefully and prayerfully that Jesus Christ is their Savior and Lord are baptized and received into membership in a Mennonite church. This is called believers' baptism." —From a pamphlet entitled "Who are the Mennonites," by La Vernae Dick. Produced by the Heritage Committee of the General Conference Mennonite Church, Box 347, Newton, Kans.

"Now according to the biblical understanding, the Holy Spirit is not a mysterious sort of something or other—and no end of damage has been done by translating the phrase as 'Holy Ghost.' The Holy Spirit is God, nothing more or less than the God we meet in any other way, place, or situation. However, he is God met in such close, intimate contact that his love, power, grace, and joy become operative in and through the most personal experience of the believer and his caravan community. And baptism is the celebration of the believer's initial entrance into this experience (the Lord's Supper is the celebration of its continuance)." Vernard Eller, *In Place of Sacraments* (Grand Rapids, Michigan: Eerdmans, 1972), p. 53.

"Conversion to God summons, leads, drives and impels to baptism, to its human confirmation in the human sphere. In baptism as a reflection of the divine work and word to which a man responds with his conversion, he confesses not only before God but also before the community and all men that, humbly awaiting its confirmation by God, he will give this answer to the best of his ability. In baptism the community also confesses that it acknowledges him as one who will give this answer to the best of his ability. In baptism the community and the candidate together establish a fact by which they are ready to be committed on all the common way ahead of them." Karl Barth, *Church Dogmatics,* vol. V, part 4, fragment (Edinburgh: T. & T. Clark, 1969), p. 145.

FOR FURTHER READING

Henry Poettcker, *A Study of Baptism.* Newton, Kans.: Faith and Life Press, 1963.

Rollin Armour, *Anabaptist Baptism.* Scottdale, Pa.: Herald Press, 1966.

Vernard Eller, *In Place of Sacraments: A Study of Baptism and the Lord's Supper.* Grand Rapids: Eerdmans, 1972.

Like living stones be yourselves built into a spiritual house, to be a holy priesthood, to offer spiritual sacrifices acceptable to God through Jesus Christ. 1 Peter 2:5

Some Christians hesitate to associate with the church because they are critical of it. It is not difficult to be critical. In two thousand years of history the church has gone in many different directions. There are literally hundreds of different denominations, including several dozen kinds of Mennonite groups. Each denomination promotes its particular emphasis—sometimes a certain style of worship or a special doctrinal emphasis. In many cases there is cooperation between churches in various projects. But in other cases there is prejudice between various groups. In the past it has even happened that members of one church group have persecuted the members of another group, supposedly for the sake of the truth of the gospel.

In the face of this diverse picture we are led to ask, Why the church? Is it a worthwhile institution? Does it serve a good purpose? Should I join it? love it? give my life for its causes? We can shed some light on our questions by describing the original reasons for the birth of the church. This may help us to see its purpose for today.

Jesus, the Founder of the Church

It is sometimes said that when Jesus was on earth, He did not start a church. This is true in one sense. He attended the existing religious institutions of the day—the temple and the synagogue. It appears that He intended to preach and teach His message in these time-honored institutions. At the same time, He also taught in homes and in the out-of-doors, in towns, and in the countryside. Wherever He went, people gathered to hear Him. The idea of teaching in the synagogue did not turn out well, since very early in His ministry He was driven from the synagogue in His hometown of Nazareth (Lk. 4:28, 29). In time, the official representatives of the temple also turned against Him (Jn. 11:55-57). Thus Jesus found himself pushed out of the "church" of the day.

At the same time, the formation of a community of believers was high on the agenda of our Lord. He did not assume that each person would relate individually to Him but that they should become a group. Indeed He commanded His disciples to "love one another" (Jn. 15:12). This commandment is the basis for what we call the church.

Thus we can say that the church serves to express the love of Jesus among its members. When He was about to face His trial and death in Jerusalem, Jesus prayed to the Father that His followers would be united in the world even though He would leave them in body (Jn. 17). He expressed the desire to His Father "that they may all be one" (17:21). The unity of Jesus with His Father was to be the model for the unity of those who believe in Christ. Jesus prayed "that they may be one even as we are one, I in them and thou in me, that they may become perfectly one. . ." (17:22, 23). Thus the church is a group of believers who have banded together in order to express among themselves the love that flows between the Father and His Son, Jesus Christ.

The first Pentecost is looked upon as the beginning of the church. Following the inbreak of the Holy Spirit (Acts 2:1-4) and the fiery preaching of Peter (2:14-36), those who believed repented and were baptized. Thereupon they gathered together for instruction, fellowship, communion, and prayer (2:41, 42). From Jerusalem the church spread to Asia Minor and, finally, to the ends of the earth.

The Church as Spiritual Family

In the Christian's experience, baptism is followed by church membership. As we pointed out in the last chapter, the two should not be separated. Baptism is the gateway to church membership. To become a member of the church is to join in a family relationship. I recall that on the day of my baptism my older brother shook my hand and said, "Welcome, Brother, into the church." This comment made me aware of the fact that I was now joining the church family. It reminded me that there was a similarity and also a difference between the parental home that my brother and I had grown up in, and the larger church family that I was joining. I was his "brother" in a new way now. The church is a spiritual family of "brothers and sisters" who belong together because they recognize a common Father in heaven, and a common Lord, Jesus Christ. The church family often includes members of the same family of relatives (the biological family), but it draws a wider circle, including all persons who are "born of God." By joining a specific local congregation we are affirming our membership in this larger family of God.

The church provides a "family" home which, in some ways, is a broader context than can be offered by the nuclear family. In the New Testament, the church is referred to as the family of God. Jesus set the stage for this when He said, "For whoever does the will of my

Father in heaven is my brother, and sister, and mother" (Mt. 12:50). In 1 Peter the believers are invited to "be . . . built into a spiritual house" (2:5). Thus the church is the context for a new family relationship that transcends the ties of race, clan, and nation. There are times when we realize that the nuclear family cannot supply all our needs or meet our expectations. In the larger church family there are resources that offer help, encouragement, and consolation at these times.

The Church in the World

The purpose of the church is to show the love of Christ to the world. The unity of the church, expressed in love, is not an end in itself. It serves fellow members of the church, but beyond that it has a larger purpose. Jesus prayed that there may be love among the believers "so that the world may know that thou [the Father] hast sent me and hast loved them [all people] even as thou hast loved me" (Jn. 17:23). We must bear in mind that Jesus was referring here to persons outside of the circle of disciples, many of whom were hostile to all that He had said and done. And yet Jesus prayed that these people would be won to Him through the attitude of love. Here we strike at the heart of the church's witness.

We should see the church not only as a gathered group, but also as a scattered extension of the community. Jesus gathered His disciples around Him for instruction and for prayer. But He also sent them into the world. His last words were "You shall receive power when the Holy Spirit has come upon you; and you shall be my witnesses in Jerusalem and in all Judea and Samaria and to the end of the earth" (Acts 1:8). The witness of the church in all sectors of society can be understood as the extension of the church into areas of need. Whenever and wherever the works of Christ and the words of Christ are being expressed, the Christian church is present. It is important to note that witness includes both word and deed. Thus the church's evangelistic ministry and its ministry of social service go hand in hand. Every member of the Christian church should seek opportunity to contribute to the mission of the church in some way, whether this is in the home or in the wider community. It is the goal of the church to spread the good news about Jesus Christ to all corners of the earth.

The Nurturing Community

The church offers the opportunity for spiritual growth and support among like-minded believers. The earliest group of believers "devoted themselves to the apostles' teaching and fellowship, to the breaking of bread and the prayers" (Acts 2:42). If we take our Christian commitment seriously, we find that we cannot pursue our goals alone. Our own thinking is too limited as a basis for understanding and applying the Christian faith. A community of people helps us to understand biblical passages and to decide upon good courses of action. Furthermore, each Christian believer has special contributions to make to fellow believers. God has endowed us with gifts that serve the entire community and individual members within it.

The activity of searching and learning becomes important within the framework of spiritual growth. Some people have the idea that baptism and church membership represent the end of a process of learning. After that we can level off. This is a wrong conception. While we gain many facts and impressions about the Bible in childhood and early youth, there is still much more to learn. Our best learning occurs in the midst of experiences in which we test our beliefs, in that period of life when we can become faithful disciples of Jesus Christ.

The church provides a meaningful context for worship. As such, it nurtures our devotion to the Lord. It is important that Christians worship God on a regular basis and in the company of like-minded believers. Since God is invisible, His presence can quickly be forgotten in day-to-day living. The Sunday morning worship service provides a regularized opportunity for worship. Through singing, the reading of Scripture, prayer, and the preached word, we communicate with God; we speak to Him and He speaks to us. The presence of other Christians in the worship service heightens the emotional element of worship and strengthens the basis of our faith in God. To be sure, there is a time and place for private worship, but it cannot adequately replace the contagious experience of public worship. The admonition of Paul to the Colossians applies today as well: "Let the word of Christ dwell in you richly, teach and admonish one another in all wisdom, and sing psalms and hymns and spiritual songs with thankfulness in your hearts to God" (Col. 3:16).

The Church in History

The history of early Christianity leaves no doubt in our minds as to the importance of the church institution. Immediately after Pentecost (Acts 1) the new followers of Christ organized a group for the purpose of worship and service. As the good news about Jesus' resurrection spread, new groups were formed in the cities and towns surrounding Jerusalem. Within a few decades church groups were located in such places as Ephesus, Corinth, Philippi, and even Rome. In time a certain amount of internal organization became necessary for the purpose of preaching, teaching, and serving needs in the community. The church's various ministries helped the new Christians to "walk worthy" (1 Thess. 2:12, KJV) of their new-found faith.

The church has had a long and checkered history of almost two thousand years. During this period there have been numerous high points and also low points. Perhaps one of the most unfortunate events occurred in the year A.D. 313, when the church made a compromise with the emperor Constantine. While this brought a period of outward peace to Christians, it also meant that the church lost much of its power to be in the world but not of the world. With this compromise the church tended to become a support base for the wishes of the state.

During the Middle Ages the church expanded its influence in all directions, mainly under the activity of the monastics. The Middle Ages saw the founding of schools for the promotion of religious training. Unfortunately the church also became involved in numerous military struggles during this time. The rise of the power of the pope at Rome was regarded negatively by many toward the end of the Middle Ages.

For this and other reasons a major religious upheaval occurred in the sixteenth century. Led by Martin Luther in Germany, Calvin in Geneva, and Zwingli in Zurich, the Protestant church came into being. Out of this struggle the Anabaptist-Mennonite movement arose as well. This latter movement should not simply be regarded as Protestant, since its earliest leaders reacted not only against Roman Catholic but also against the Protestant Reformers. A recent book by Walter Klaassen characterizes the Anabaptists as "neither Catholic nor Protestant."

An important emphasis of the Anabaptists was that the church must be a visible body of committed disciples of Christ. In this connection they upheld adult baptism and mutual caring for one another.

During the last four hundred years the Protestant church as well as the churches of Anabaptist origin have gone in many and various directions. As present-day believers who love the church, we are saddened by certain divisions within the church. At the same time the variety of denominations, insofar as they live peaceably with one another and support mutual causes, can be viewed as a witness to the rich variety of gifts that God has bestowed upon His people.

TOPICS FOR DISCUSSION
1. The biblical view of the church as the people of God.
2. The importance of the church as a realistic earthly community, yet with an ideal heavenly vision.
3. The church as family and fellowship.
4. The church's mission: What is it?
5. What can you gain from and offer to the church?

SELECTED SCRIPTURE PASSAGES
John 17
Ephesians 4
1 Peter 2:9, 10

AIDS TO REFLECTION

"The central task of evangelism is forming disciple communities. Evangelism is not simply saving individuals from hell for heaven, nor inviting them to repentance and then leaving them to struggle alone to be faithful to their confession that Jesus is Lord. Evangelism is calling men and women to repentance and inviting them to become a part of the community of God's people which participate even now and here on earth in the kingdom of God which will finally come in all of its fullness." John Driver, *Community and Commitment* (Scottdale, Pa.: Herald Press, 1976), p. 90.

"The church is an event, a happening that Christ brings about from day to day. We have no promise that Israel will be faithful, that we can look at the given institution called church and say that it represents the purpose of Christ for history. We have only the promise that Christ will be faithful and that as he works in history there will always be a remnant who have not bowed the knee to Baal nor surrendered to the limited ways of the world. We have no promise that even these faithful will resist the temptations. We have only the promise that his call will come again and again to die to the false forms of the world and to rise with him to the journey to his free future." Colin W. Williams, *The Church* (Philadelphia: The Westminster Press, 1968), p. 48f.

"The Spirit makes the believer a part of Christ's body. It is he who creates the unity of this body, which consists of many members, with different gifts of the Spirit (cf. 1 Cor. 12). By becoming a part of Christ through the Spirit, the believer guarantees his pneumatic existence. Not only does God assure the believer, through his Spirit working in the risen Christ, of eternal life in the *present*—since the resurrection of the crucified Christ means a final victory over death; but also God will, through the same life-giving Spirit, give him eternal life in the *future* too." Hans Küng, *The Church* (Garden City, N.Y.: Image Books, 1976), p. 222.

FOR FURTHER READING

C. Norman Kraus, *The Community of the Spirit.* Grand Rapids: Eerdmans, 1974.
Harold S. Bender, *These Are My People.* Scottdale, Pa.: Herald Press, 1962.
Franklin H. Littell, *The Anabaptist View of the Church.* Boston: Starr King Press, 1952.

13/WORSHIP AND SERVICE

"You shall love the Lord your God with all your heart, and with all your soul, and with all your strength, and with all your mind; and your neighbor as yourself." Luke 10:27

The two most important activities of the Christian are worship and service. The purpose of worship is to foster a right relationship toward God; the purpose of service is to ensure a proper relationship to fellow human beings.

While on earth, Jesus taught us to practice both of these aspects of Christian life. On one occasion He was asked by a lawyer, "Teacher, which is the great commandment in the law?" He answered, "You shall love the Lord your God with all your heart, and with all your soul, and with all your mind. This is the great and first commandment. And a second is like it, You shall love your neighbor as yourself" (Mt. 22:36-39). When Jesus was tempted by Satan in the wilderness, He sent the devil away with these words from the Old Testament: "You shall *worship* the Lord your God and him only shall you *serve*" (Mt. 4:10, italics mine). In His own ministry Jesus served His neighbors by healing the sick, feeding the hungry, encouraging the discouraged, and giving guidance to the misguided. He also attended services of worship at the temple and in the synagogues. At times He withdrew to a quiet place to pray. It is significant that at the most critical time in His life of service, on the evening of His trial and death, Jesus went to the Garden of Gethsemane to pray. This is our model for an integrated life of service and worship.

Worship of God

The English word *worship* means "worthship." When we worship God, we show our respect for Him. We recognize Him as the Creator, and ourselves as creatures; we acknowledge Him as the Giver of all good things, and ourselves as receivers of His blessings. In worship we tell the Lord what He is "worth" to us. This has the effect of helping us gain a true estimate of ourselves in relation to God.

We are constantly tempted to worship false gods. These false gods appear in a variety of forms. Sometimes we attempt to ascribe supreme "worthship" to our very own selves, or to some friend whom we admire above all else, or to some material possession such as clothing or a car. We are constantly in danger of ascribing supreme worth to persons and things around us, thus creating false gods. The practice of the worship of God on a regular basis, if done sincerely, can help us to maintain a singular devotion to the one and only God, and consequently keep earthly things in their proper place.

Worship can be practiced in a variety of settings, each with its own unique value. The Sunday morning worship service in the church provides opportunity for worship in the context of community. Persons of all generations are represented in the congregational gathering. Furthermore, Sunday morning worship is usually well planned beforehand, and in many cases makes use of artistic forms of expression such as liturgies, beautiful hymns and anthems, and prepared sermons. This heightens the possibility of meaningful worship in some ways.

However, the congregational worship service cannot meet all of our needs and desires for worship. Much can be gained from a deeply personal and individual relationship with God. Private prayer and meditation, both on a regular basis and spontaneously "when the spirit moves," also have their place in the life of the Christian. To a significant extent our lives are not and cannot be public. A portion of our lives is influenced by private concerns and impressions. Our Father in heaven can serve as a constantly available Companion who shares this private world with us and helps us to gain perspective upon our individual experiences of successes and failures.

Midway between the large congregational gathering and an individual walk with God there is also the opportunity for the experience of worship in small groups. Jesus said, "Where two or three are gathered in my name, there am I in the midst of them" (Mt. 18:20). In the small group setting it is possible for each person to share expressions of praise and need. It is encouraging to see that in our day small groups in the church are flourishing. At the same time the importance of the larger congregational gathering should not be undervalued. Both have their place in the practice of Christian worship.

One of the subtle temptations we should resist is that of finally worshiping the very form of worship which we find meaningful. For this and other reasons it is important that we worship God in a variety of ways and places.

Worship of Christ

Interpreters of the New Testament sometimes carry on a debate as to whether or not one should worship Jesus. Some say worship belongs to God, while obedience belongs to Jesus. Others would advocate worship of both the Father and the Son. The point that Jesus must be obeyed in life rather than worshiped is sometimes stressed because there may be a tendency among Christians to miss the point that Jesus is not only the object of our emotional affection, but is also to be taken seriously as our example in daily living.

It is unfair to downplay the worship of Christ unduly. If we begin with the definition of worship as the affirmation of Christ's "worthship," then we can freely include Him as the object of our worship. At His birth, the angels, the shepherds, and the wise men recognized His great "worth" and worshiped Him. And while it is significant that during His lifetime Jesus sometimes cautioned would-be worshipers against adoring Him in the course of His earthly ministry (Mk. 10:18), the writer of the Book of Revelation invites us to worship Christ as our crucified and resurrected Lord: "Worthy is the Lamb who was slain, to receive power and wealth and wisdom and might and honor and glory and blessing!" (Rev. 5:12.) We are invited to worship Christ insofar as this inspires us to follow Him in life and to await our final union with Him in resurrection.

Prayer

We began this chapter with the statement that worship and service are the two most important aspects of the Christian life. Prayer has its place within this scheme. Prayer is conversation with God. It is somewhat helpful to compare prayer to a conversation with your best friend. God is like a friend in whom we can confide. In faith we can assume that He understands us and that He is deeply interested in our welfare. There is an important difference, however, between a conversation with a friend and conversation with God. Unlike a visible friend, God cannot be seen or heard. For this reason the conversation is sometimes one-sided; we see and hear only ourselves. Thus if we want to hear God speak to us, we must tune ourselves to a somewhat different expectation than is possible in human conversation. What are some of the ways in which we hear God speak?

First and foremost, He has spoken to us (1) through His Son, Jesus Christ. We have a record of the words and deeds of Jesus in the

Gospels. These give us specific clues as to how God speaks to us. Furthermore, (2) the entire Bible is seen by Christians as the Word through which God speaks to us. While it is not always a simple matter to decide which parts of the Bible were meant only for the past and which parts are applicable as well for today, it is possible, through careful study and prayerful reading, to "hear" the word of God communicated through the entire Scripture.

Besides Jesus Christ and the Scriptures, one can list many other media through which the "voice" of God becomes known to us. The early Christians emphasized the importance of the word of God which comes (3) through the community of believers, the church, as persons speak to one another in that context and as leaders address the entire group. (4) The very course of history, with its ongoing sequence of events, also provides a medium through which God makes His will known. We must not claim that the course of history as such constitutes the voice of God. Nevertheless, there are important events which speak of His will and way. Finally, there are the (5) very personal experiences of individuals. God is able to speak through events which occur in our lives, through our minds, through our senses, through the emotions of our hearts, through memory, through imagination, and through the thoughts of others.

In conversing with God, patience is an important virtue. Most often God does not answer our prayers immediately. He takes His own time and encourages us not to become anxious. In fact, some of our prayers will only find their answers on the other side of death.

The most important prayer and the prayer we should utter most frequently is "Lord, may Thy will be done." This prayer helps the Christian to place desires and life directions into a broader perspective. An alignment needs to occur between our desires and the desires of God. Sometimes our desires will be affirmed by the divine Spirit. At other times they will be transformed or even called into question. To pray that "Thy will be done" is to commit ourselves to a process in which we gain a sense of direction from God from day to day.

Discipleship

One of the most frequent invitations which Jesus extended to His hearers came in the words "Follow Me." Whoever responded to the invitation for any length of time was counted as one of His disciples. The word *disciple* literally means "learner." The word is also closely related to the word *discipline*. We know that in order to learn something well, it takes discipline. Sometimes we exercise self-discipline in order to learn our lessons; sometimes it requires discipline from outside of ourselves. Jesus expected that those who followed Him would submit themselves to Him as students in a classroom. Unlike our formal settings, however, His classroom was mobile; His students followed Him throughout the countryside, learning their lessons along the way. In the course of His ministry He made clear to His disciples that He had come to serve mankind and that He expected His followers to imitate Him in their service. Thus discipleship includes service as well as discipline.

The kind of service that Christians are called to participate in includes a wide range of involvements. On a very basic level, it is a matter of assuming a Christian attitude in all of life's relationships. It is always easier to follow one's natural desires or a "spur of the moment" decision than to consciously relate a Christian life-style to all daily tasks. The Apostle Paul encouraged the early Christians at Thessalonica to "lead a life worthy of God" (1 Thess. 2:12) as they went about their daily work. This would apply to Christians in whatever work they are engaged, whether as students, as housewives, as carpenters, as lawyers, etc. It is a matter of relating to one's day-to-day associates in a spirit of Christian love and of following a code of ethics which applies Christian principles in all decisions. A Christian attitude of discipleship is not to be reserved only for special occasions, but takes effect continuously, whether in the home, at school, at work, or at play.

There are also special times and places when Jesus' invitation to discipleship becomes particularly crucial. Following the clues that Jesus left us, we can say that it is the disciple's special obligation and opportunity to take up the cause of the weak and the downtrodden. Jesus made a point of identifying with persons in His day who were often despised by society (such as tax collectors and sinners) or who were in great need (the blind, the lame, the sick). This tells us that we should also make special efforts in our day to contribute our resources of time, energy, and money to help people with special needs. It is significant that throughout history and in the present day the church has often led the way in helping individuals and groups of persons who are the victims of natural disaster, social pressure, or war. The Salvation Army, Mennonite Central Committee, Mennonite Disaster Service, World Vision, and Church World Service are only a few examples of church organizations which seek to follow Christ in this way.

The Anabaptist Vision of Discipleship

Harold S. Bender, the twentieth-century Mennonite historian, wrote an essay about Mennonite beginnings in which he claimed, on the basis of his research, that *discipleship* (German: *Nachfolge*) was the word that characterized the Anabaptist predecessors of the Mennonites most accurately. Central to their theology was the idea that to be a Christian means to be conformed to Christ not only in doctrine, but also in life. Of the many attempts by students of the Anabaptist-Mennonite tradition to characterize this movement, Bender's conclusion has gained the widest acceptance.

The earliest Mennonites of the sixteenth century did not say that the Christian could earn salvation by following Christ. They believed in Jesus Christ as their Savior from sin. However, they added that forgiveness is of little effect and the grace of God is cheapened if it is not followed by Christian discipleship. In the sixteenth century Menno Simons characterized true faith in the following way:

A genuine Christian faith cannot be idle, but it changes, renews, purifies, sanctifies, and justifies more and more. It gives peace and joy, for by faith it knows that hell, the devil, sin, and death are conquered through Christ, and that grace, mercy, pardon from sin, and eternal life are acquired through Him. In full confidence it approaches the Father in the name of Christ, receives the Holy Ghost, becomes partaker of the divine nature, and is renewed after the image of Him who created him. It lives out of the power of Christ which is in it; all its ways are righteousness, godliness, honesty, chastity, truth, wisdom, goodness, kindliness, light, love, peace.[1]

In the church of today there are signs of faithfulness to the Anabaptist vision and to the original vision which Jesus sought to instill in His disciples. Here and there individuals and institutions are seeking to express Christian discipleship in the world. At the same time, there is a widespread tendency to "sell out" to the *status quo* of society on the one hand, and on the other to a brand of Christianity which emphasizes an inner peace and grace at the expense of a social concern and a rigorous application of the love of Christ in all relationships of life. Each generation of Christians is invited anew to take up the cross and follow Jesus Christ the Lord.

TOPICS FOR DISCUSSION
1. The value of worship for ascertaining life direction.
2. The importance of corporate worship.
3. Increasing our awareness of God and neighbor through prayer.
4. Making discipleship specific and practical as a community of believers and as individual Christians.

SELECTED SCRIPTURE PASSAGES
1 Timothy 3:1-13
2 Corinthians 8
John 15
Matthew 6:1-21
Mark 14:12-31

AIDS TO REFLECTION
"It doesn't take much imagination to realize that a basic consecration to God turns into a consecration to other people." Gordon G. Talbot, *Overcoming Materialism* (Scottdale, Pa.: Herald Press, 1977), p. 58.

"The Christian's chief emotion Godward is an emotion of love. Love is shown partly by faith and by giving of one's self completely in surrender and obedience. However, there is also a direct outpouring of love in worship. Worship is communion with God in which we allow God to speak to us and in which we respond with gratitude, devotion, and a desire to please Him." Lloyd L. Ramseyer, *The More Excellent Way* (Newton, Kans.: Faith and Life Press, 1965), pp. 33f.

"First and fundamental in the Anabaptist vision was the conception of the essence of Christianity as *discipleship*. It was a concept which meant the *transformation of the entire way of life* of the individual believer and of society so that it should be *fashioned after the teachings and example of Christ*. The Anabaptists could not understand a Christianity which made regeneration, holiness, and love primarily a matter of intellect, of doctrinal belief, or of subjective 'experience,' rather than one of the transformation of life. They demanded *an outward expression of the inner experience.* Repentance must be 'evidenced' by newness of behaviour." Harold S. Bender, "The Anabaptist Vision," in *The Recovery of the Anabaptist Vision,* edited by Guy F. Hershberger (Scottdale, Pa.: Herald Press, 1957), p. 42.

"Cheap grace is the preaching of forgiveness without requiring repentance, baptism without church discipline, Communion without confession, absolution without personal confession. Cheap grace is grace without discipleship, grace without the cross, *grace without Jesus Christ, living and incarnate.* Costly grace is the treasure hidden in the field; for the sake of it a man will gladly go and sell all that he has. It is the pearl of great price to buy which the merchant will sell all his goods. It is the kingly rule of Christ, for whose sake a man will pluck out the eye which causes him to stumble, it is the call of Jesus Christ at which the disciple leaves his nets and follows him." Dietrich Bonhoeffer, *The Cost of Discipleship* (New York: The Macmillan Company, 1959), p. 36.

FOR FURTHER READING

John W. Miller, *The Christian Way.* Scottdale, Pa.: Herald Press, 1969.
Elizabeth O'Connor, *Journey Inward, Journey Outward.* New York: Harper, 1968.
Guy F. Hershberger, editor, *The Recovery of the Anabaptist Vision.* Scottdale, Pa.: Herald Press, 1957.

14/FAMILY

Have we not all one father? Has not one God created us? Why then are we faithless to one another, profaning the covenant of our fathers?
Malachi 2:10

The most important institution in human life is the family. In a simple, yet profound, sense our very being depends upon the existence of the family. A mother and a father brought us into this life; a parental home sustained us. We would be nonexistent if there were no family or no possibility of family life.

The family is also an important aspect of Christian life and thought, and the Bible contains some important theological teachings about the family.

All in the Family

Our thinking about the family must begin where Genesis begins—with the whole of creation and with all mankind. Anyone who has lived, is living, or will live in the future is a descendant of the first man and the first woman. Thus whether people recognize it or not, every person on the face of the earth is related to every other person on the earth. Furthermore, we all stem from the creative act of God. Thus all people upon the earth are children of God and brothers and sisters of one another.

The emphasis upon the all-inclusiveness of the family of God is expressed here and there throughout the Bible. Following the account of the Fall of mankind, the Bible looks forward in hope to a time when all people will confess that God is Lord of His great family. In the call of Abram the promise was given that "all the families of the earth [shall] be blessed" (Gen. 12:3, KJV). The promise was made again to Jacob that by him and his descendants "shall all the families of the earth be blessed" (Gen. 28:14, KJV). Years later the Prophet Isaiah saw the vision of a time when "many peoples" (family tribes) shall join the "house of Jacob" (the family of Israel) and be taught by God to walk in the ways of the Lord (Is. 2:3). In the New Testament, the church is referred to as a family which was being built into a "spiritual house" (1 Pet. 2:5) composed of people from many nations. The vision of a world-encompassing family is expressed in Ephesians 3:14-21—"For this reason I bow my knees before the Father, from whom every family in heaven and on earth is named . . . that you, being rooted and grounded in love, may have power to comprehend with all the saints what is the breadth and length and height and depth, and to know the love of Christ. . . ."

To state that God is the Creator of all mankind, and that all people belong to one united family, is obviously not a description of what is happening or has ever happened totally in the world. Not everyone confesses belief in the Lord God as their Creator-Parent; nor do all people everywhere express brotherly and sisterly love toward one another. The ideal relationship between the children of God was already marred by the sin of our first parents. Yet unity in love still remains our responsibility and our goal. It is our duty to regard and to serve our world-neighbors in the spirit of divine goodwill.

If people took this idea seriously, it could have a revolutionary effect upon our way of life. To treat one another as members of the same family calls into question our national boundaries, our racial prejudices, our class distinctions, our denominational biases, and our individualistic way of life. It would affect our vocations and professions in that our work in the world would be seen as a service to family members. The food we produce on our farms feeds our larger extended "family." How could we possibly wage war against a neighboring nation, since we belong to the same family?

The fact that many people upon our earth are not inspired by the vision and hope of family love should not prevent us from promoting our hope. We have the calling from God to live peaceably with all inhabitants of the earth, and to pray that the promises of God may be incarnated in communities of care and hope.

The Church Family

The Christian hope for the salvation of God's potential people is kept alive by a special family within the family of mankind. All who have committed themselves to Jesus Christ and to membership in the Christian church comprise a special family. Ideally the church family should be a reflection of God's intention for everyone. Love and service to those within and without are the ideal characteristics of the church. In the church family there can be no distinction between first- and second-class citizens, no competition between the intelligent and the not-so-intelligent, no preference of male over female, no antagonism between old and young, no preference of the physically strong over the handicapped. All have an equal share in the grace of the Father and in fellowship with Jesus Christ and with one another. All are in the family.

It is a special event for the church when young people express their allegiance to the church family. With the teenage years one's attachment to the parental home tends to lessen. Whereas in childhood we were quite dependent on mother and father, during the high school years a need for independence begins. There comes a shift of interest as we scan the horizon for other possible attachments. The church family should appeal to us as "a group worth trusting." It represents a broader circle of people than our immediate family circle, while at the same time often including our family members. Many young people find persons of the same age and older persons in the church who listen to their problems and aspirations and express an attitude of genuine caring and acceptance. At the same time, one can find some of the typical family conflicts in the church as well. It is our challenge and duty to build the church family into a community of love.

The Biological Family

Where would we be today if we would not have had the advantages of a family context in which a mother and a father cared deeply enough for us to provide the physical and spiritual necessities of life? To be sure, there are exceptional stories of persons who have "made it" through life in spite of the early death of their parents or the sheer neglect of a mother or a father. However, the natural and preferable context for growth is a home where we are surrounded with the parental protection and care of a loving father and mother.

The importance of the family is assumed from the beginning of creation. In Genesis 1:27 we read that the Creator made mankind as male and female. In Genesis 2:24 we read that it is good for a man to leave father and mother at a certain time and devote himself to a wife. Thereafter it is reported that children are born to Adam and Eve, the first man and woman. We should note, however, that the Bible speaks of the earthly family in broader terms than we might think. When we use the word *family* we think of the nuclear family—father, mother, and the immediate children. In our thinking, this would be the basic family unit. However, in the Bible the extended family is the basic unit. This includes all relatives such as grandparents, grandchildren, uncles, aunts, cousins, nieces, and nephews. Anyone who has "common blood" belongs to one family or tribe. Perhaps you have wondered why there are so many genealogies in the Bible. These lists preserve the roots of the family from generation to generation. It was believed that the very perpetuation of the family from one generation to the next is proof of the love and steadfastness of God.

The emphasis upon the family, which is found especially in the Old Testament, is by no means outdated. There are periods in life, especially in youth, when we tend to become critical of parents and relatives. However, it is not right for us to allow a negative attitude to fester. The fifth commandment encourages children to honor father and mother. This law applies not only to little children, but to grown children as well. In fact, some biblical scholars say that this commandment is written especially to older "children," encouraging them to take responsibility for their aging parents and grandparents.

While one's responsibility to the extended family is highlighted in the Scriptures, the importance of the husband-wife union is also emphasized. The decision to marry a life partner should not be made lightly or for the wrong reasons. It is important, therefore, that young people think carefully about their relationships with persons of the opposite sex during the period of dating and courtship. The marriage promise is intended to hold for life; thus one must be quite certain of this step. Common sense would tell us that the prospective marriage partners should be of like faith, since it is presumed that all of life will be affected by one's faith commitment.

In the scriptural view, the marriage bond is the proper God-ordained context for sexual intercourse. It is against the will of God to make use of the sexual act outside of marriage. Physical union of male and female is ordained for the conception of children and as an expression of singular ultimate human love.

Furthermore, it is preferable that children be raised in the context of two adults, a father and a mother. Before a married couple commit themselves to the conception of children, husband and wife should consider seriously the responsibility this implies. It is unfortunate if parents separate and leave the children with one of the adults. The basis for a caring relationship to one's children is assured when a sense of genuine love and responsibility has been established to a significant level between marriage partners. It is well to begin to establish this basis before one's children are born.

It should be said quite emphatically that while marriage is an institution blessed of God, singleness belongs to the will of God as well. Whether one remains single by design or by circumstance, life can be as fulfilling for persons who remain single as for those who marry.

The key to a successful marriage relationship is expressed in Ephesians 5:21—"Be subject to one another out of reverence for Christ." It is not a matter of deciding who will have the upper hand in the marriage arrangement. Rather, the partners enter into a covenant as equals. Together the marriage partners place themselves under the lordship of Christ in service to one another, to the church family, and to mankind. The family unit must not turn inward but must see itself as a part of the larger family of God.

The Mission of the Family

Just as there are many problems that beset the society of our day, so also the family is plagued with serious problems. All around us there are instances of child neglect, tension between husband and wife, conflict between parents and children, disrespect for the aged, discrimination against single adults, and abuse of the God-given sexual gift. Unfortunately, families in the Christian church are not unaffected by these negative trends, since we live in the midst of society. However, it is the mission of the family unit and of its individual members to show the world a better way. It is the task of the family to be a sign of the purpose of the heavenly Father for His children upon the whole earth.

TOPICS FOR DISCUSSION
1. Biblical perspectives on the term *family.*
2. The church family as the "spiritual" family surrounding individuals and nuclear families.
3. The Christian definition of love.
4. The importance of love and order in sexual relations.
5. Applying the New Testament lists of "virtues" to our family relationships.

SELECTED SCRIPTURE PASSAGES
Proverbs 1 to 7
1 John 4:13—5:2
Ephesians 5:21—6:4

AIDS TO REFLECTION
"In the wonder and ultimate mystery of love, spiritual truths come alive; they take on flesh-and-blood reality by being incarnated in persons. Encountering the being of one's partner—really seeing and experiencing that unique person—is a deeply moving spiritual meeting, spirit with spirit." Howard J. and Charlotte H. Clinebell, *The Intimate Marriage* (New York: Harper & Row, 1970), p. 186.

"In Genesis 3 we are not dealing with the order of creation as God made it or intended it—although some quite mistakenly believe this to be the case. Chapter 3 represents an order that resulted from Adam and Eve's rebellion against God. This rebellion resulted in a marring of God's intended order through the 'curses' found in chapter 3. These curses, like the curse we saw in Genesis 8, do not picture the ideal social order but rather a fallen order. For God's ideal for men and women, we need to look at Genesis 1 and 2 where we read that male and female were created alike—in God's image—and given the same tasks." Perry and Elizabeth Yoder, *New Men New Roles* (Newton, Kans.: Faith and Life Press, 1977), pp. 43f.

"Who hates his neighbour has not the rights of a child. And not only has he no rights as a child, he has no father. God is not my father in particular, or any man's father (horrible presumption and madness!), no, he is only father in the sense of father of all, and consequently only my father in so far as he is the father of all. When I hate some one or deny that God is his father—it is not he who loses, but me: for then I have no father." Soren Kierkegaard, *Journals* (Magnolia, Mass: Peter Smith Publisher, Inc., 1959).

FOR FURTHER READING
John W. Miller, *A Christian Approach to Sexuality.* Scottdale, Pa.: Herald Press, 1973.

David R. Mace, *The Christian Response to the Sexual Revolution.* Nashville: Abingdon Press, 1970.

Letha Scanzoni, *Men, Women, and Change.* New York: McGraw-Hill, 1976.

Helmut Thielicke, *The Ethics of Sex.* New York: Harper & Row, 1964.

15/BEING MENNONITE

For no other foundation can anyone lay than that which is laid, which is Jesus Christ. 1 Corinthians 3:11

Mennonites present a very diverse picture to those who look at us from the outside. What is a Mennonite? Some would say Mennonites are persons who dress plainly and live in communities. Others would point out that Mennonites drive horses and buggies or paint the chrome on their cars black. Someone else would say Mennonites are good farmers and good cooks. Others would say they are reserved and keep to themselves. Still others would say Mennonites are Fundamentalist Christians. Some would point out that Mennonites are known for their voluntary service to people in need. Opinions depend very much on what the public has read in the newspapers or what contact they have had with Mennonite groups.

Within the Mennonite fold there is also a good deal of diversity of opinion as to who we are. Some would consider Mennonites as just another arm of the Protestant church. Another typical recent view is that Mennonites are to be characterized as restoring the true church which Jesus had in mind when He gathered His disciples. Still others see Mennonites as essentially a group with certain cultural emphases, due to Swiss or German descent. A recent book on the Mennonites in Kansas characterizes the Mennonites there as "a people of two kingdoms," with one foot in the world and the other in the kingdom of God.[1]

Being Mennonite will always mean different things to different people. The essential point is that we appreciate our rich heritage. One way to cultivate an appreciation of the Mennonite church is to taste the flavor of the original events that provided the inspiration for the Mennonite movement. This takes us back to the Reformation of the sixteenth century.

Mennonite Beginnings

The Mennonites trace their origin to the Reformation of the sixteenth century. In the first half of that century, Martin Luther, Ulrich Zwingli, John Calvin, Conrad Grebel, Menno Simons, and others influenced many people to break with the Roman Catholic church. Their stated intention was to return to the teachings of the New Testament.

Among the early Reformers were a group of radicals who held that Luther and Zwingli were not taking their reform measures far enough. Luther had dreamed of creating a church composed of only those who were committed, but he compromised by allying his movement with the German princes, thus again creating a territorial church as the Catholics had. The radicals called for a church that was free of geographical and governmental boundaries. Zwingli, a Reformed leader in Zurich, had initially committed himself to a reform that would be based solely upon scriptural teachings. But when it came to reforming the practices of baptism and the Lord's Supper, he drew back. A more daring group of Reformers were prepared to take the Reformation to its logical conclusion. The key figures in the radical group were Conrad Grebel, Felix Manz, and George Blaurock.

This small nucleus began to meet regularly in a private home to study the Scriptures, to discuss their convictions, and to pray. They were quite aware that their meetings would incur the wrath of church and state. Yet they persisted. On the night of January 21, 1525, the group was once more meeting in secret, when they came to the conviction that they should form a new fellowship. George Blaurock asked Conrad Grebel to rebaptize him. (He had been baptized as an infant.) Grebel complied. Blaurock then baptized the others upon their request.

With this move, a new church was born. It was committed to believer's baptism and to the separation of church and state. The brethren were also prepared to suffer for their new-found convictions. And suffer they did! Both Catholics and the newly organized Protestants persecuted these Anabaptists (meaning rebaptizers). Many died a martyr's death.

Although persecution pursued the earliest Anabaptists, the movement spread rapidly. Hans Denck introduced the movement to central Europe. Hans Hut attracted converts in Bavaria, Swabia, Franconia, and Moravia. Balthasar Hubmaier preached the new message in Austria. Pilgram Marpeck served mainly in south Germany. Michael Sattler served the group in Switzerland and south Germany. Behind each of these names there is a dramatic story of faithfulness and persecution.

In the Netherlands the movement touched a Catholic priest by the name of Menno Simons. Through his own reading of the Scriptures, Menno had already begun to raise questions about the Catholic practice of the Lord's Supper and baptism. In 1536 he united with the Anabaptist Reformers. For twenty-five years he served the emerging church through preaching and writing. Menno Simons was a respected and stabilizing influence during these early years.

In the year 1545 a governmental decree issued against Menno Simons and his followers used the term *Mennist* to refer to those who followed Menno's teachings. The name stuck, and today the term *Mennonite* designates a large body of Christian believers whose historical tradition is traced back to the radical Reformers of the sixteenth century.

Anabaptist-Mennonite Convictions

The following is a brief summary of the Anabaptist-Mennonite understanding of Christian faith and life.

1. *Biblical authority.* The Scriptures are accepted as the final authority in matters of faith and life. The teachings of Jesus provide the key for an understanding of the Scriptures.

2. *Regeneration.* The Christian life has its beginnings in the conscious decision to accept the forgiving grace of Jesus Christ as a basis for a new walk.

3. *Discipleship.* The decision to believe that Jesus Christ is Savior leads directly to a life of discipleship under the lordship of Christ.

4. *Church membership.* The church is a community of believers formed on the basis of a voluntary commitment. Believer's baptism is the symbolic expression of a commitment to the church, the visible body of Christ.

5. *Mutual caring.* It is the duty of the church and its members to submit to the exercise of redemptive discipline. Members of the fellowship express mutual concern for the welfare of one another.

6. *Worldwide mission.* The love of Christ compels every disciple to obey the Great Commission. This includes ministry to all in the name of Christ through the evangelistic word and the caring deed.

7. *Suffering love.* Radical discipleship expresses itself in a life of peace and nonresistance.

The General Conference Mennonite Church

Since the beginning of the Mennonite tradition in Europe in the sixteenth century, a variety of Mennonite groups have developed. These are now spread throughout almost the entire world. At times new groups have formed due to missionary activity. At times division within the church has caused new groups to arise. At other times immigration has resulted in new beginnings. The movement of Mennonites to various corners of the earth has been inspired by persecution, by missionary and service outreach, by a search for better living conditions, and sometimes by the desire to protect a conservative way of life.

The General Conference Mennonite Church is the second largest Mennonite body in North America. This denomination had its beginnings in Pennsylvania, where a young schoolteacher, John H. Oberholzer, along with several other brethren in the (Old) Mennonite Church, insisted upon certain changes. They advocated the dropping of the collarless ministerial coat, a written constitution, publishing a catechism, Sunday schools, mission work, and free association with other denominations. The General Conference body had its beginnings at West Point, Iowa, on May 28, 1860, where three like-minded congregations organized.

Since that date many individual churches and groups of churches have joined the General Conference. This includes a great many nineteenth- and twentieth-century immigrants from Russia, Prussia, Poland, and Switzerland. A large proportion of General Conference members have their roots in the groups which migrated from the Netherlands to Prussia to Russia to the United States, Canada, and South America. The General Conference has also extended its borders to countries such as India, Africa, Japan, and Taiwan, through missionary effort. Today there are 99,000 or more members who participate in, or are related to, General Conference programs around the world.

The conference is not bound together by a common creed. While there is a general statement of faith, the binding factor is the common work of missions and service, as well as the opportunity for fellowship at the triennial conference and in smaller circles at other times. The basic unit is the local congregation. The conference is seen as a fellowship of local autonomous congregations. The larger body is able to undertake some tasks which local groups could not do alone. These include the implementation of mission programs, the production of educational curricula, organizing a voluntary service program, support in church planting, and publishing a church paper. The General Conference readily cooperates with other Mennonite groups in such ventures as

Mennonite Central Committee, Sunday school curriculum production, and seminary education.

Conclusion

Some years ago the word *Mennonite* was not a respected term in society. But through the efforts of our people and by the grace of God, the Mennonite church has gained respect around the world. We can be thankful for our heritage!

TOPICS FOR DISCUSSION
1. What it means to be called a Mennonite: our history, our beliefs, our opportunities.
2. Why Mennonites are "neither Catholic nor Protestant."
3. Our worldwide horizons: facts and implications.
4. Coming to grips with our Mennonite customs.
5. The recovery of the Anabaptist vision in our day.

SELECTED SCRIPTURE PASSAGES
Luke 12:32-34
1 Corinthians 3:11
Luke 9:23-27

AIDS TO REFLECTION
"Our sustained efforts at conforming ourselves to our culture have paid off handsomely. Along with most other christians we have been effectively immunized against the acceptance of our radical heritage. We have domesticated the church; we have invested heavily in solid real estate and continuing institutions, and we continue to do so. We have willingly put on the straightjacket of authoritative theologies. In many ways we have given away our birthright for a bowl of soup. But many Mennonites now know what we have done. Unlike Esau, who begged for return of his birthright 'to the point of tears' and was still rejected, we can buy back into ours. Many other christians, whose spiritual ancestors persecuted our fathers, are now investing heavily in our birthright." Walter Klaassen, *Anabaptism: Neither Catholic nor Protestant* (Waterloo, Ont.: Conrad Press, 1973), p. 83.

"Looking to the black church, Mennonites will gain insight into the way blacks experience God at the feeling level. The black church worship patterns include elements of openness, free style encounter with God, and celebration of life. Worship in the black church tradition is a creative experience, not a book slavishly followed or a ritual rehearsed. The quietness, the apparent serenity, the supposed orderliness of worship in white Mennonite churches often serve to cover up a spiritual hollowness and narrowness that perpetuate the status quo and undergird racism." Hubert L. Brown, *Black and Mennonite* (Scottdale, Pa.: Herald Press, 1976), p. 95.

"Alone of all the churches of the Reformation, the Anabaptists considered evangelism as belonging to the essential being of the church." John H. Yoder, "The Prophetic Dissent of the Anabaptists," *The Recovery of the Anabaptist Vision*, edited by Guy F. Hershberger (Scottdale, Pa.: Herald Press, 1957), pp. 97f.

FOR FURTHER READING

Walter Klaassen, *Anabaptism: Neither Catholic nor Protestant.* Waterloo, Ont.: Conrad Press, 1973.

Fritz Blanke, *Brothers in Christ.* Scottdale, Pa.: Herald Press, 1961.

John Richard Burkholder and Calvin Redekop, editors, *Kingdom Cross and Community.* Scottdale, Pa.: Herald Press, 1976.

Samuel Floyd Pannabecker, *Open Doors: A History of the General Conference Mennonite Church.* Newton, Kans.: Faith and Life Press, 1975.

16/PEACE

"You have heard that it was said, 'You shall love your neighbor and hate your enemy.' But I say to you, Love your enemies and pray for those who persecute you, so that you may be sons of your Father who is in heaven." Matthew 5:43-45a

131

Mennonites are known throughout the world for their position of nonresistance. They do not advocate participation in war. Instead they emphasize a gospel of love and promote constructive, rather than destructive, service in the world. From the earliest beginnings of our denomination, its leaders have understood that the message of peace is an essential ingredient of the good news.

In September of 1524, shortly after the earliest beginnings of the Anabaptist movement, Conrad Grebel, the leader among the Swiss, wrote, "True, believing Christians are as sheep in the midst of wolves. . . . They use neither the worldly sword, nor engage in war, since among them taking human life has ceased entirely, for we are no longer under the Old Covenant."[1] Felix Manz, another early leader of the Anabaptists, said, "No Christian smites with the sword, nor resists evil."[2] The Dutch Mennonites chimed in with their Swiss brethren. Dirk Philips wrote, "The people of God arm themselves not with carnal weapons . . . but with the armor of God, with the weapons of righteousness . . . and with Christian patience, with which to possess their souls and overcome their enemies."[3] Menno Simons wrote, "The regenerated do not go to war, nor engage in strife. They are the children of peace . . . and know of no war. They render unto Caesar the things that are Caesar's and unto God the things that are God's. Their sword is the sword of the Spirit which they wield with a good conscience through the Holy Ghost."[4]

Alongside of the refusal to go to war, the Anabaptists emphasized positive Christian love. The idea of love appeared quite often in their writings. When questioned about his position, Felix Manz said that "Christian and brotherly love requires that everyone is bound to show love to his brother in the open."[5] Early in 1527 another Anabaptist leader in central Germany wrote that God has given man His law in a new form, the form of love. The earliest Mennonites saw man not only as a sinner, but also as a person who has been given the capacity to love the neighbor. Such love is expressed not only in emotional ways, but also in the sharing of worldly goods. Some of the early Anabaptists took this to mean that Christians should live in communities in which they shared all things in common. Thus the Hutterite community was begun early in our history. Others continued to live in the midst of society but sought to put the ideal of love into practice in the world.

Participation in government and, more particularly, the warfare of nations has been the testing ground for the Mennonite stand on nonresistance. The Anabaptists recognized the necessity of government and saw the state as ordained by God. But its task was to maintain order and promote the good in the sub-Christian aspects of society. The Schleitheim Confession of 1527 puts it this way: "The sword is ordained by God outside the perfection of Christ." As far as disciples of Christ were concerned, Mennonites have traditionally held that they were not called to engage in war. Rather, their efforts should be toward overcoming evil with good and, as much as is possible, encouraging all persons in society to do the same. How could someone who seeks to be conformed to the image of Christ practice revenge and take human life?

Mennonite history from earliest times until now is rich with examples of persons and groups who have witnessed courageously to the gospel of peace in the midst of nationalistic military enterprises and civil wars. It can be said that while we have not always understood the doctrine of nonresistance in the best possible way, many of our forebears have paid a high price for the right to exemption from military service. At the same time, it must be admitted that our history is also spotted with numerous examples of compromise in the face of difficult situations.

What the Bible Teaches About Peace

Does the Mennonite position on nonresistance have a solid basis in the Christian faith? Or is it just an extra which we can take or leave? Since the Anabaptists based their views on their understanding of the Scriptures, we must ask whether peace and nonresistance are central to the Bible.

Before the birth of Christ, Zechariah, the father of John the Baptist, spoke of Jesus as One who would "guide our feet into the way of peace" (Lk. 1:79). When Christ was born in Bethlehem, the angels who brought the news to the shepherds said, "Glory to God in the highest, and on earth peace among men with whom he is pleased!" (Lk. 2:14.) Later in His ministry Jesus said, "Blessed are the peacemakers, for they shall be called sons of God" (Mt. 5:9). Further, He taught: "Do not resist one who is evil. But if anyone strikes you on the right cheek, turn to him the other also" (Mt. 5:39). Also, He said, "Love your enemies and pray for those who persecute you" (Mt. 5:44). At the end of His ministry in the Garden of Gethsemane, when Peter raised his sword in a last effort to protect Jesus against the soldiers who had come to take Him captive, Jesus said to him, "Put your sword back into its place; for all who take the sword will perish by the sword" (Mt. 26:52). The climax of Jesus' teaching about nonresistance came when, hanging on the cross, He prayed for His persecutors: "Father, forgive them; for they know not what they do" (Lk. 23:34). We can affirm without hesitation that nonresistance and the peace teaching were essential ingredients in the life and teachings of Jesus.

There is another side to the words and deeds of Jesus. On one occasion He said, "Do not think that I have come to bring peace on earth; I have not come to bring peace, but a sword" (Mt. 10:34). Is Jesus advocating war? It becomes evident in the context that the reference is to the fact that because of His radical call to discipleship, some members of families will need to leave their loved ones for the cause of Christ. There will be divisions within families because of the call to faithfulness. Thus the gospel is a "sword" which divides family loyalties. On another occasion toward the end of His ministry, Jesus entered the temple and saw how the courtyard was being abused by businessmen. He became quite irritated at the sight and proceeded to drive out those who were carrying on trade there (Mk. 11:15). Some have claimed that Jesus was contradicting His own nonresistant stand on this occasion. However, we should understand His act as prophetic indignation against an activity which had no place in the house of God. Following this outburst, Jesus taught the people as follows: "Is it not written, 'My house shall be called a house of prayer for all the nations'? But you have made it a den of robbers" (Mk. 11:17). Thus we can conclude that while Jesus was an advocate of the way of peace, He spoke a prophetic word of judgment against evil when and where it was warranted.

These last observations tell us that for the Christian, peace does not mean the absence of conflict. Rather, the word of peace seeks to penetrate difficult situations and speak its message in the midst of turmoil. It is a matter of standing in the crossfire between warring parties and speaking the word of peace in both directions, to both sides. This is a dangerous position, but it is the way of Christ. The Mennonite people have expressed this more difficult stand in their service programs around the world.

While we sometimes have the impression that the Old Testament is largely filled with stories of bloodshed, a basis is already laid there for the gospel of peace which we find in the New Testament. In the first chapter of Genesis, man is reported to be created in the image of God (Gen. 1:27). This means, among other things, that his purpose upon earth is to further the creative activity of the Lord rather than to destroy aspects of the created order. Furthermore, if man as such is created in the image of God, then we have no right to destroy another person, since that would involve the destruction of godliness which is imprinted in our fellow human beings. We also read in Genesis 1:28 that man is called to "be fruitful and multiply and fill the earth and subdue it." To engage in warfare would be to work against this calling. The unstated, yet underlying, idea in creation is that the resources of the earth have been given to mankind so that we might explore the resources of the earth in order to serve one another cooperatively. To plunder, destroy, maim, and kill other people upon the earth is contrary to this creative purpose of God.

Responsibility for the care of one another is emphasized in the story of Cain and Abel. It was expected that Cain would be his brother's keeper. Instead he killed him. This displeased the Lord greatly, and He punished Cain.

In the story of Lot and Abram we have a simple, yet important, story of a peaceful attitude. Abram wished to avoid strife between Lot and himself over the question of a parcel of land. In a spirit of peace he said to his nephew, "If you take the left hand, then I will go to the right; or if you take the right hand, then I will go to the left" (Gen. 13:9).

One of the Ten Commandments reads, "You shall not kill" (Ex. 20:13). Unfortunately this commandment was applied to the people of Israel, but not to the surrounding nations. According to Israel's understanding, it was permitted in certain instances to declare war against non-Israelites. This is a difficult section of the Old Testament to understand. On the one hand, it appears as though God were encouraging the Israelites to attack their surrounding neighbors so that they could possess their promised land and protect themselves. On the other hand, there were voices among the people, especially the prophets, who spoke of a coming kingdom of peace when all nations would learn the way of peace from the people of Israel. (See Is. 2:2-5.)

It becomes evident in the New Testament that the warfare and laws of vindication ("An eye for an eye and a tooth for a tooth") of the Old Testament were not the will of God. Jesus said, "You have heard that it was said, 'An eye for an eye and a tooth for a tooth.' But I say unto you, Do not resist one who is evil" (Mt. 5:38, 39). Furthermore, He said, "You have heard that it was said, 'You shall love your neighbor and hate your enemy.' But I say to you, Love your enemies and pray for those who persecute you" (Mt. 5:43, 44). Thus we see progression from certain parts of the Old Testament to the New Testament. The old way of warfare and vindication is to be left behind, and a new understanding of the will of God now takes its place.

Justice

The biblical teaching about peace is integrally related to the theme of justice. Peace between persons and among nations is not thought of in terms of withdrawing from the neighbor. Rather, peace is promoted in the interest of service. We are to seek the good of our fellow beings rather than to harm them. We are to love our neighbors as ourselves. Rather than conquer the neighbor's land and possess it for ourselves in order to accumulate wealth, we are to share our abundance with others, and to promote the distribution of property and the necessities of life so that all can partake of the blessings provided through God's created order.

When Jesus walked this earth, He found injustice among people in many areas of daily life. Still today the rich get richer and the poor get poorer. People who have positions of strength tend to use this to their advantage and thus mistreat those who are weak in our society. There is conflict between people of different races. Jesus encountered the same problems in His day. Self-righteous religious Pharisees gave the Samaritans and Gentiles little chance to prove their worth in society and before God. When Jesus died on the cross, He broke down the dividing wall of hostility (Eph. 2:14). As far as He was concerned, the ground was level at the foot of the cross. Everyone had equal access to Jesus Christ. This meant that henceforth we should no longer carry prejudice in our hearts and in our actions. Our love for all mankind and our practice of justice toward all is henceforth expressive of the fact that the grace of God is not for a chosen few, but is available equally to everyone.

It is difficult to live this way both in good times and in difficult times. In good times we forget our responsibility all too quickly. In difficult times we are prone to compromise in order to "save our skins." Yet we must challenge one another in the Christian church to be faithful. This means, first, that we cannot go to war, although to take this stand may mean to suffer at the hands of government. We can be thankful if allowance is made for exemption from war. Secondly, this means also that we must practice an active life of service in times of peace as well as in times of war. Voluntary service programs through the Mennonite Central Committee and other church agencies provide opportunity for service. But let us not overlook the fact that every vocation in which the Christian is found also provides an opportunity for involvement in active justice. Peace and justice begin at home.

A Final Thought

The Christian message of peace is three-dimensional. It includes peace with God, peace with oneself, and peace with one's neighbors. At the same time, the three dimensions are inseparable. Inner peace and peace with others is based on peace with God. Similarly, one can claim to have peace with God only if one has also sought to live in peace with all mankind.

TOPICS FOR DISCUSSION
1. Peace as an integral part of the good news of Jesus Christ.
2. The biblical idea of peace; its broad application.
3. Justice and righteousness among all people as the will of God.
4. The Mennonite peace witness: its glory and shame.
5. Peace witness in your life.

SELECTED SCRIPTURE PASSAGES
1 Corinthians 13
Romans 12
Matthew 5

AIDS TO REFLECTION

"I am no doctrinaire pacifist, but I have tried to embrace the pacifist position as the lesser evil in the circumstances. I do not claim to be free from the moral dilemmas that the Christian non-pacifist confronts, but I am convinced that the church cannot be silent while mankind faces the threat of nuclear annihilation. If the church is true to her mission, she must call for an end to the arms race." Martin Luther King, *Strength to Love* (New York: Harper & Row, 1964), p. 171.

"Because he has his own war to wage, the Christian breaks completely with the earthly strategy of physical combat. If the Christian is to be true to the Lord Jesus Christ, he must make a full break with the ancient and ultimate apostasy. His weaponry is not the belligerent word of ultimatum issuing in the thrust of the sword that divides, destroys, and perpetuates the very evil he is seeking to eliminate. His weaponry is rather the persuasive word of the gospel issuing in compassionate concern for liberation, reconciliation, and celebration of the approaching Christ-ordained age of peace." Jacob J. Enz, *The Christian and Warfare* (Scottdale, Pa: Herald Press, 1972), p. 88.

"True Christian believers are as sheep among wolves, sheep for the slaughter; they must be baptized in anguish and affliction, tribulation, persecution, suffering and death. They must be tried with fire, and must reach the fatherland of eternal rest, not by killing their bodily but by mortifying their spiritual enemies." Conrad Grebel, "Letters to Thomas Müntzer," in *Spiritual and Anabaptist Writers,* edited by G. H. Williams (Philadelphia: The Westminster Press, 1957), p. 80.

"The Prince of peace is Christ Jesus; His kingdom is the kingdom of peace. . . . His Word is the word of peace; His body is the body of peace; His children are the seed of peace; and His inheritance and reward are the inheritance and reward of peace. In short, with this King, and in His kingdom and reign, it is nothing but peace." Menno Simons, "Reply to False Accusations," in *The Complete Writings of Menno Simons,* edited by J. C. Wenger (Scottdale, Pa.: Herald Press, 1956), p. 554.

FOR FURTHER READING

138

Jacob J. Enz, *The Christian and Warfare.* Scottdale, Pa.: Herald Press, 1972.
John Howard Yoder, *Nevertheless.* Scottdale, Pa.: Herald Press, 1971.
Frank H. Epp, *A Strategy for Peace.* Grand Rapids: Eerdmans, 1973.

"I am the Alpha and the Omega, the first and the last, the beginning and the end." *Revelation 22:13*

Does life have any meaning? This is the haunting question that everyone asks in one way or another. The question of life's meaning is asked in a deeply personal way by each individual: What is the value of *my* life? The question is also asked about the sweep of history and the universe as such: Does this vastness of space and endless progression of time have any purpose at all?

Thus far in this book our answer to this question has tended to be existential. We have stressed the importance of faith and faithfulness here and now. Our Teacher, Jesus Christ, placed great emphasis upon a living faith which does not get bogged down in a bygone past or in a future that has not yet arrived. In one sense the present moment is all we have and all we need.

At the same time, we know that our present space and time belong to a larger whole. The little space each of us occupies is part of a vast universe that stretches farther than man can imagine. Each moment of time contributes to a history that comes from an incomprehensible past and flows into an endless future. Thus we cannot help but ask the question of meaning in its greatest possible dimensions.

The broader question of the meaning of life and history is raised by our very life experiences. The miracle of birth at the beginning of life leads us to ask, Why was I born? The impending fact of death at the other end raises the same question. A beautiful experience in the midst of life causes us to ask, Can this moment be preserved forever? Tragic events of history raise the question of why the earth and its inhabitants were brought into being in the first place and where history will eventually drive us.

Life Has Ultimate Meaning

Our biblical faith offers important answers to the question of life's meaning. First, we affirm on the basis of Genesis 1 and 2 that the earth and the surrounding universe were created for a divine purpose. Nor did God give up on His goal when man fell. He continues to work in the universe for the good of mankind.

Christian faith affirms the moral character of the universe. That is, all life has value. This means that whatever happens falls eventually under the judgment of God upon evil and the blessing of God upon the good. Jesus said: "For as the Father has life in himself, so he has granted the Son also to have life in himself, and has given him authority to execute judgment, because he is the Son of man. Do not marvel at this; for the hour is coming when all who are in the tombs will hear his voice and come forth, those who have done good, to the resurrection of life, and those who have done evil, to the resurrection of judgment" (Jn. 5:26-29). These words prevent us from thinking that in the end God might simply annihilate everything, or on the other hand, that God will close His eyes to evil and bless all of life and history as His will.

Through the cross and resurrection of Jesus Christ the Father has announced to us the defeat of the evil powers of the universe and the triumph of the good. This is what is meant when we read that "he has put all things under his feet" (Eph. 1:22). This truth is experienced in the realm of faith and hope more than as actual evidence around us here and now. The resurrection is only a foretaste of the final defeat of evil. When the risen Lord was about to ascend to heaven, two messengers announced, "This Jesus, who was taken up from you into heaven, will come in the same way as you saw him go into heaven" (Acts 1:11). The reason for His coming again is to accomplish finally the purpose of God in His creation. Because God values life, He will fulfill His purpose through history.

Personal Life After Death

"If a man die, shall he live again?" (Job 14:14a.) Most persons ask this question at some point in the course of life. For the Christian, the answer is "yes." This affirmation is based upon our understanding of God. God is a God of promise and of fulfillment. He intends to achieve the goals He has set for us and for himself. And yet many of life's episodes end without fulfillment. We look forward to an adventurous camping trip, but sickness interferes. We anticipate a growing friendship, but someone else interferes. Many times the promises of life do not find their fulfillment in the here and now. This is especially true where death cuts short the achieving of God's good goals. It is also evident when we study the way in which many stages of history fall short of the achievement of divine purpose. If bad is bad, then we must conclude that the promises of God will find their fulfillment beyond death. It is of the nature of God to fulfill His promises. He will not allow half-achievements. Thus it is appropriate that the Apostle Paul wrote, "If for this life only we have hope in Christ, we are of all men most to be pitied" (1 Cor. 15:19).

Hope and trust rest on a foundation which transcends the experiences of this life. We anticipate fulfillment in a life beyond death.

The resurrection of Jesus is the promissory sign of our personal resurrection. With the resurrection of Christ, God vanquished the greatest enemy that overpowers us—death. In the course of life we often struggle with powers that seek to play havoc with our well-being. Psychological problems, temporary sickness, a difficult relative, a faithless friend, or even a material force such as wind and weather threaten our existence. The strongest threat imaginable is death itself, which overcomes every person. But Christ has put death under His feet. Thus we know that death can be overcome and we need not fear any lesser power. The only fear we have is fear itself.

How we conceive of resurrection from the dead is important. A resurrection is not a resuscitation—that is, a mere reviving of our earthly bodies. A revived body, as in the case of Lazarus, would only die again after a few years. Nor should the resurrection be thought of in the Greek sense of the separation of body and soul, with the body deteriorating and the soul rising to immortality in a bodiless existence. Rather, the resurrection is best characterized as the resurrection of the person in a new body, a "spiritual body" (1 Cor. 15:44) which is incorruptible. It is the God-intended "person" in us that is resurrected to new life, but in a new body. Thus there will be some continuity and some discontinuity between this life and the next. To some extent, we will be the same person; to some extent, we will be different.

Final Events

Among Christians there are many differing ideas concerning the events of the end of time. These are based mainly on an interpretation of certain passages of the Bible, mainly the Book of Revelation. This book makes mention of the millennium (20:1-10), a period of one thousand years, which precedes the final triumph of Christ. Among those who take the millennium literally, there are two schools of thought: the premillennial view and the postmillennial view. Premillennialism holds that there will be a final period of world history which will last for one thousand years. At the beginning of this period all living Christians will be "caught up" with Christ. During the thousand years that follow, the world will be under the sway of evil and the Antichrist. At the end of this period of time the Lord will win a victory against the Antichrist, who will be destroyed. There will be a resurrection of the dead and a judgment. Thereafter the lordship of Christ will be established forever.

The view known as postmillennialism differs from premillennialism in that it places the first return of Christ at the end of the millennium rather than at the beginning. Thus it is sometimes held by postmillennialists that we are living in the millennium now. They see certain events in history as well as the presence of evil upon earth as a sign that we are moving toward a critical final onslaught between the forces of good and the forces of evil. Christ is expected to return at the end of this great battle. With His return He will rescue the faithful and resurrect the dead. There is one version of postmillennialism which says that the world will get better and better during the millennium. This will prepare the way for the somewhat natural advent of Christ.

A third view, known as amillennialism, does not accept the idea of a millennium in the sense of a literal period of one thousand years. Rather, the millennium is a symbolic term, referring to the blessedness of the Christian experience here and now and to the intermediate state of believers after death. Amillennialism holds that at the end of history Christ will return in glory. At this time the forces of wickedness will be vanquished and the saints who have died, as well as those presently living, will join Christ in heaven as the redeemed host. Hell is prepared for the devil and his followers. There has been a tendency among Mennonite theologians to favor the amillennial view.

What Shall We Believe About the End?

We make a mistake if we structure our view of the end of history too tightly. Some of what we read in the Bible should be understood symbolically. A symbol points to a very real event, but we cannot always know the exact outline or facts of the event in question. For example, the term *millennium* refers to an age or stage of history, but the term may have been used only to signify a long period of time, not necessarily a period of exactly one thousand years. For us, the exact facts are not as important as the assuredness that the event will occur in reality.

The Christian vision of our final goal is variously depicted in Scripture. The end is understood as a time when "the earth shall be full of the knowledge of the Lord" (Is. 11:9); the stage of history when "Thy will be done, On earth as it is in heaven" (Mt. 6:10); the moment when "we all attain to the unity of the faith . . . to the measure of the stature of the fulness of Christ" (Eph. 4:13); the creation of a "new heaven and a new earth" (Rev. 21:1); the day when Christ will finally sanctify and cleanse the church and present it to himself a glorious church "without spot or wrinkle" (Eph. 5:25-27).

In the midst of this maze of symbolism we must bear in mind that the future of life remains in part a mystery until it arrives. In 1 Corinthians 13:12 we read, "Now I know in part; then I shall understand fully." What we can know assuredly is that our Lord and Savior, Jesus Christ, has preceded us and is preparing the way for our entry into His final peaceable kingdom. In the meantime we have the opportunity here and now to express the characteristics of the promised coming kingdom by worshiping God and loving one another.

How Shall We Live?

The Christian church needs to have a theology of hope. We cannot live with our eyes only upon the pages of past history, or only with an attachment to the present. The future also belongs to our quest for the meaning of life. A future hope in God provides nurture for the present. We remain faithful to God in good times and in evil times because we believe that the future is in the care of our heavenly Father. Thus the Christian's future hope is an inspiration for faithful living in the present.

TOPICS FOR DISCUSSION
1. The biblical message of hope, based upon the Creator, promise, Jesus Christ, and faith.
2. Images of hope in Scripture.
3. Personal hope in the face of tragic world events and personal discouragements.
4. Signs of hope in present life.

SELECTED SCRIPTURE PASSAGES
Isaiah 35:1-10
John 11:17-27
Revelation 21 and 22
1 Corinthians 15
Matthew 25

AIDS TO REFLECTION
"We pray to Thee, O Christ, to keep us under the spell of immortality. May we never again think and act as if Thou wert dead. Let us more and more come to know Thee as a living Lord who hath promised to them that believe: 'Because I live, ye shall live also.'

"Help us to remember that we are praying to the Conqueror of Death, that we may no longer be afraid nor be dismayed by the world's problems and threats, since Thou hast overcome the world.

"In Thy strong name, we ask for Thy living presence and Thy victorious power. Amen." Peter Marshall, *Mr. Jones, Meet the Master* (Westwood, New Jersey: Fleming H. Revell, 1949), p. 151.

"This world is not the heaven of self-realization, as it was said to be in Idealism. This world is not the hell of self-estrangement, as it is said to be in romanticist and existentialist writing. The world is not yet finished, but is understood as engaged in a history. It is therefore the world of possibilities, the world in which we can serve the future, promised truth and righteousness and peace. This is an age of diaspora, of sowing in hope, of self-surrender and sacrifice, for it is an age which stands within the horizon of a new future. Thus self-expenditure in this world, day-to-day love in hope, becomes possible and becomes human within that horizon of expectation which transcends this world. The glory of self-realization and the misery of self-estrangement alike arise from hopelessness in a world of lost horizons. To disclose to it the horizon of the future of the crucified Christ is the task of the Christian Church." Jurgen Moltmann, *Theology of Hope* (London: SCM Press Ltd., 1967), p. 338.

"In the Bible it is the nature of the almighty God to ceaselessly create unheard-of things. Who then but he should be able to make all things new in such an abundant way as is indicated in the metaphorical talk about the resurrection of the dead? If the resurrection was previously an image of human longing and imagination, it could now become the goal of confident hope. For the Christian, this hope is not just a matter of some indefinite future; the path to it has been opened by Jesus' resurrection, thus by that reality of Jesus which encountered the disciples after the catastrophe of his crucifixion." Wolfhart Pannenberg, *What Is Man?* (Philadelphia: Fortress Press, 1970), pp. 52f.

FOR FURTHER READING

Jurgen Moltmann, *Theology of Hope.* London: SCM Press, 1965.

Paul Erb, *Bible Prophecy: Questions and Answers.* Scottdale, Pa.: Herald Press, 1977.

Russell Aldwinckle, *Death in the Secular City.* Grand Rapids: Eerdmans, 1972.

Louis Berkhof, *The Second Coming of Christ.* Grand Rapids: Eerdmans, 1953.

Footnotes

Chapter 3

[1]Gordon D. Kaufman, *Systematic Theology* (New York: Charles Scribner's Sons, 1968), p. 102.

Chapter 11

[1]*The Schleitheim Confession*, tr. and ed. by John H. Yoder (Scottdale, Pa.: Herald Press, 1977), p. 10.

[2]Quoted from *The Mennonite Encyclopedia*, vol. III, p. 394.

Chapter 13

[1]Menno Simons, "True Christian Faith," in *The Complete Writings of Menno Simons*, J. C. Wenger, ed. (Scottdale, Pa.: Herald Press, 1956), p. 396.

Chapter 15

[1]James Juhnke, *A People of Two Kingdoms* (Newton, Kans.: Faith and Life Press, 1975).

Chapter 16

[1]Quoted in J. C. Wenger, ed., *The Doctrines of the Mennonites* (Scottdale, Pa.: Mennonite Publishing House, 1952), p. 35.

[2]*Ibid.*

[3]*Ibid.*

[4]*Ibid*

[5]Robert Friedmann, *The Theology of Anabaptism* (Scottdale, Pa.: Herald Press, 1973), pp. 70f.